THE ENTREPRENEUR'S MINDSET

THE ENTREPRENEUR'S MINDSET

How to Rewire Your Brain for Business Success

M. Lalia Helmer

Copyrighted Material

The Entrepreneur's Mindset: How to Rewire Your Brain for Business Success

Copyright © 2021 by M. Lalia Helmer. All Rights Reserved.

No part of this publication may be reproduced, stored in a retrieval system or transmitted, in any form or by any means—electronic, mechanical, photocopying, recording or otherwise—without prior written permission from the publisher, except for the inclusion of brief quotations in a review.

M. Lalia Helmer
www.laliahelmer.com
linkedin.com/in/laliahelmer

ISBN: 978-1-7369387-0-6 (print)
    978-1-7369387-1-3 (ebook)

Printed in the United States of America

Cover and Interior design: 1106 Design

I dedicate this book to my amazing family, the greatest source of meaning, purpose, and joy in my life.

CONTENTS

Entrepreneur	1
Duncan Logan	13
Key Strategies	25
Mindset Exercises	29
Lisa Fetterman	33
Key Strategies	42
Mindset Exercises	45
Guy Praisler	49
Key Strategies	62
Mindset Exercises	65
Greg Kimma	67
Key Strategies	73
Mindset Exercises	75
Iddo Tal	79
Key Strategies	93
Mindset Exercises	97
Shar Behzadian	101
Key Strategies	110
Mindset Exercises	113

Art Agrawal	117
Key Strategies	125
Mindset Exercises	129
Michael Coscetta	133
Key Strategies	149
Mindset Exercises	153
Conclusion	157
Acknowledgments	159
Resources	161
Biography	163

ENTREPRENEUR

You recognize the word. For most of us, these four syllables evoke a cascade of mental associations. The little girl or boy who starts a lemonade stand down the block. The techie who invents the hottest new game app. Or the style maven who launches an online fashion empire.

But have you ever found yourself wondering: Do all of these very different breeds of innovator share similar wiring in the brain? Are there specific traits or personality types, a recognizable mindset, required to start and grow a business? In other words, were these individuals *born* entrepreneurs, or did they *become* entrepreneurs?

Perhaps you might also ask yourself, "Do *I* have what it takes?" Not just the technical skills or the financial resources (which, of course, you'll need), but also the mental and emotional wiring—*the entrepreneur's mindset*, let's call it.

We derive the word "entrepreneur" from the French term meaning "to undertake." According to some accounts, the French/Irish economist Richard Cantillon introduced the concept of "a person who undertakes a risk" back in the 17th century. Other accounts attribute the term's initial use to French economist Jean Baptiste Say, who employed a designation derived from the word "*adventurer.*"

The famed Austrian economist and scholar Joseph Schumpeter later contributed pivotal theories of entrepreneurship, placing particular import on the notions of innovation and technological change. According to Schumpeter, entrepreneurs' fundamental characteristics included the following: These individuals are self-reliant; they strive for excellence and display high levels of optimism; they delight in risk-taking challenges. Schumpeter also coined the phrase "entrepreneurial spirit" *(Unternehmergeist)*, which describes an entrepreneur as being "one who does new things or does things in a new way."

Still, economists, academics, and business experts continue to debate the definition of the term *"entrepreneur."* The continued disagreement likely results from the varied range of businesses that frequently qualify as "entrepreneurial": everything from a self-employed contractor to an individual-service business, from an innovative technology company to a fast-growing start-up with unicorn potential. The matter of funding complicates any discussion of definition, too: some companies need venture funding, while others require small-business lending, and others find funding entirely on their own. You could—as Schumpeter and others have done—make the argument that a true entrepreneur is strictly one who creates an innovative business.

I take a broad and generous view of entrepreneurship. To my thinking, anyone who checks even one of the above boxes would qualify, whether they are in the field of business, science, social movements, the arts, or nonprofits. If they are innovating or creating something new, they fit the mold if they are taking risks and proving themselves an adventurer in their field. They "Think Different," in the parlance of the classic Apple advertising campaign.

You remember those ads, don't you? In print and on television, they celebrated forward-thinking icons like Mahatma Gandhi, Amelia Earhart, and John Lennon, to name just a few. They encouraged us to "Think Different," and the voice-over narration of every television commercial began with a dedication: "To all the crazy ones…" The campaign was spot-on, too—it's the crazy ones, after all, who have changed the world time and again.

I vividly recall seeing one of the "Think Different" billboards in Northern California, right along the 280 Freeway in Cupertino, when my husband and I first relocated to the area in the early 1990s. This one featured Albert Einstein, and it seemed the perfect welcome, given California's open spirit of creativity, innovation, and entrepreneurism.

No wonder, then, that I was immediately comfortable in this new environment of Silicon Valley—I have long displayed a streak of autonomy and freethinking. As a child, by the time I was five years old, my mother had labeled me "too independent," and my brothers had branded me a "crazy little girl." I was energetic and creative, determined to "do my own thing," which most certainly did not mesh well with my family's expectations or the larger society of the time.

By adolescence, I had shed the "crazy little girl" label, but others had replaced it. Suddenly, I was the nonconformist, the family black sheep. Socially, I never quite fit in with the "in-crowd." I maintained the need to follow my path, to feel and "think different." Sometimes I was too creative, other times too conservative. Wherever the crowd was marching, I wasn't in lockstep. Even at school, I would find unconventional and creative ways to execute my assignments, much to my professors' irritation. "Just do what we requested in the assignment," they would say.

By the time I reached college, I knew that my independent nature was embedded deep within my personality, and I embraced this way of being. It became a core belief, a lodestar for how I would lead my life. I remember being home during one of my college breaks and having an impassioned discussion with my father about the importance of following one's own path. According to my father, if everyone behaved that way, there would be anarchy and chaos in the world. This idea was challenging for me to understand. I wasn't advocating chaos, just craving acceptance as a freethinker. This friction, this tension, sent me on a quest. Who was I? Why was I like this? Seeking answers, I plunged into the stacks of my college library to discover the keys to my behavior, thinking, and emotions. There I found books that spanned the spectrum of psychological topics, everything from self-help to rigorous psychological theory. I supplemented that reading with introductory college psych courses, where I learned the theories of Freud, Jung, Maslow, and others.

Luckily for me, too, I met a perfect companion in my self-journey: my husband. On one of our early dates, as we were discussing individuality and self-determination, I remember thinking, Wow, this is the first person I have met who thinks about life *the same way* as I do. Little did we know in those early days of our relationship that life circumstances would carry us to a part of the world which embraced those very same ideas!

Indeed, it wasn't until we moved to California that I fully realized my interest in human psychology. By that point, I felt less inclined toward clinical work; instead, I felt drawn to a specific sub-field of applied psychology known as industrial/organizational psychology, or as some educational institutions have dubbed it, business psychology. This branch of the field develops research methods to improve human relations, leadership, and productivity within organizations. During my graduate coursework, I also studied an emerging sub-field called positive psychology and its intellectual offspring, positive organizational psychology.

Positive psychology seeks to assess the drivers of individual well-being and fulfillment. Positive organizational psychology deals with the applications of that research, enabling organizations to develop the strengths of their employees and foster positive experiences. In addition to examining matters of well-being and happiness, positive psychology seeks to identify and enumerate other positive traits, such as grit, hope, resilience, optimism, and intrinsic motivation. Discovering positive psychology during the course of my graduate work, I immediately sparked to the subject matter. From then on, I began integrating its precepts into my work in training and development, coaching, and teaching.

At just around the same time I earned my master's in organizational psychology, start-ups began cropping up, and incubators started booming. Colleges and universities began to offer entrepreneurship programs, and suddenly there was a founder on every street corner—or at least in every café! For me, the timing was wonderfully opportune. Such an environment was ideal for initiating a study into the personality and mindset of successful entrepreneurs.

That study had an organic starting point, and it was this fundamental question: Are successful entrepreneurs born, or are they made? Indeed, many such individuals show early indicators of a specific, unique, and frequently identifiable psychological makeup. Often this makeup first manifests as a disinterest in traditional academic pursuits. We know many of the giants—luminaries like Bill Gates and Mark Zuckerberg—chose to drop out of college to pursue their passions. Steve Jobs similarly dropped out of college, though he remained on campus and "dropped in" to courses that piqued his interest. Years later, in his famous commencement speech at Stanford University, Jobs gave credit to a university calligraphy course for setting the foundation of the type used in all Macs.

That last point invites the question: Why did these visionary entrepreneurs lose patience with academics? It wasn't for lack of intelligence. Instead, they each possessed an independent mode of thinking, coupled with a desire to create something new, which contrasted with the methods of most schools' reliance on standardized curriculums and rote memorization.

But what are some of the other traits inherent in the entrepreneurial personality? Only gradually are studies beginning to shed a bit more insight on this subject. In one such study, researchers utilized the most widely accepted personality-assessment model, the Big Five, to unearth commonalities among the most effective entrepreneurs and managers. The results show—not surprisingly—that entrepreneurs tend to be independent thinkers, more open to new ideas; they are creative, innovative, and achievement oriented. Also, they are more resilient, persistent, hard-working, and motivated.

In another study, researchers noted that undergraduate and MBA students with the stated intent of starting and owning their own business scored high in measures of the *Proactive Personality*. Again, no surprise there. It stands to reason that would-be entrepreneurs are more inclined to believe they have control of their environment; thus, they are more likely to take the initiative and action, and more readily identify opportunities. These results dovetail perfectly with the French definition of an "entrepreneur" as "someone who undertakes a risk."

Other studies have attempted to identify the telltale traits essential for not just the initial stages of entrepreneurial success but also for longer-term prosperity. The results point to several essential characteristics: creativity, self-reliance, ability to adapt, tolerance of ambiguity and uncertainty, commitment, and determination.

Determination and its many synonyms—perseverance, persistence, stick-to-itiveness, grit—are often cited by entrepreneurs as an essential character trait for those who seek to follow in their footsteps. Thomas Edison, one of America's foremost innovators and perhaps the most underrated of entrepreneurs, is well known for his famous quotations regarding success and failure. Everyone knows the "99% perspiration" line, certainly, but I prefer a different one: "Our greatest weakness lies in giving up. The most certain way to succeed is always to try just one more time."

Where does this determination come from, and how does it interconnect with the other essential characteristics of entrepreneurial success? Consider the example of Richard Branson, who from childhood was considered headstrong, even pigheaded. However, his parents, although worried at times, reportedly nurtured this quality. They would allow him to go off on little adventures; they encouraged him to explore the subjects of his curiosity. To this day, he credits these boyhood experiences of self-reliance with helping to hone the tenacity and "no quit" attitude that got him through many difficult periods in his fifty years of business.

Steve Jobs, for his part, viewed passion as an essential ingredient of persistence, which was itself crucial to success: "I'm convinced that about half of what separates the successful entrepreneurs from the non-successful ones is pure perseverance.... Unless you have a lot of passion about this, you're not going to survive. You're going to give it up. So, you've got to have an idea, or a problem or a wrong that you want to right that you're passionate about; otherwise, you're not going to have the perseverance to stick it through."

The actor-turned-venture capitalist Ashton Kutcher, when choosing between potential start-up investment opportunities, factors into consideration the personality of the leader. For Kutcher, the person at the helm of a start-up is more important than the idea. And the most vital trait they can possess? You guessed it—grit. That's the deciding factor. You can get a firsthand example of this kind of grit by reading Iddo Tal's interview in the pages ahead. Not surprisingly, Kutcher invested in Tal's company.

Why does creating entrepreneurial businesses require such grit and mental toughness, you might ask? Consider the fact that almost half of all new businesses fail within the first five years. And during those tumultuous years, entrepreneurs face seemingly endless challenges: raising enough funding, finding the right partner, building the right team, achieving the right sort of product/market fit, among countless other issues. In later stages, too, entrepreneurs will have to worry about exit strategies, scaling problems, legal issues (look no further than Uber and Airbnb for prime examples), investor relationships, not to mention the threat of being fired from their own company. Such unending tribulations require an astonishing level of perseverance, as each new day brings daunting obstacles, risks and uncertainty, messiness and chaos.

And the risks I have mentioned above are merely the business-related ones. Consider also the darker psychological risks that often accompany entrepreneurship. Overwhelmed by the constant specter of failure and lacking in the correct psychological tools, the entrepreneur can face unhealthy work/life balance, stress, anxiety, sleep disorders, failed relationships, depression, and, yes, even suicide. How best to mitigate these adverse effects? It certainly helps to have the right psychological toolkit, one that creates the mindset necessary for the entrepreneur to start and grow their enterprise.

To chart the reaches of the entrepreneur's mindset, I have drawn upon research in positive and social psychology to develop my questions. My interview subjects are a varied bunch. As you'll see, they run the gamut from an entrepreneur at the very early stages of idea development to the founder running a multinational business. One of the founders I interviewed was an Uber driver who, needing the extra cash, picked me up on my way home from SF. I have even included a former consultant to entrepreneurs.

Their aspirations are diverse, too: Some of them are looking to change the world, while others are just aiming to build a profitable business based on their ideas and inspirations. I chose them because I saw them as examples of having the ideal entrepreneur's mindset.

As you can imagine, they are a busy lot. I conducted my interviews anywhere I could pin them down for a few precious moments of their time, while drinking green smoothies in their workspace or coffee lattes at an SF café. I even snatched phone interviews on Sunday afternoons using my trusty iPhone Call Recorder app.

While the questions are mostly similar from person to person, the answers are unique and exceptional. I was particularly struck by their self-awareness and their self-leadership in maintaining optimism, self-confidence, and resilience. In our conversations, I heard about how they deal with stress, how they approach risk, and how they view failure. I learned how they set goals, how they utilize their strengths, and how they contend with weaknesses.

Each of these entrepreneurs offers specific personal strategies and guiding philosophies; they reveal the support systems that helped them pull through the turmoil. Their answers range from the philosophical—like Lisa Fetterman's belief that "the obstacle is always the way"—to the practical, like Guy Praisler's admonishment to "put on your sneakers, go out, run, take a good shower." We even encounter a bit of the profane when Art Agrawal describes how he tries to get the "sh*t out of my head."

Maybe you have already failed at a business, or perhaps you are about to launch a business but don't feel you have "what it takes" to get started and keep going. If so, then there's good news: You don't have to be "born" an entrepreneur.

The latest research suggests that inheritance accounts for only slightly more than 50% of any individual's personality and mindset. The rest comes from an acquisition. You can, quite literally, teach yourself new behaviors and thought processes. Neuroscientists have studied the brain's neuroplasticity and have found that the right mental exercises, strategies, and habits can shape new behaviors, emotions, and attitudes. They can help us hone our creativity and innovative thinking; they can help us manage stress and even endow us with flexibility and open-mindedness. In other words, you can develop an entrepreneur's mindset, or hone an existing one, to help you navigate your challenges.

As you page ahead, you will get a unique opportunity to hear from each of these entrepreneurs in their own words. Every chapter is a self-contained interview, including both the questions and the answers. At the end of each chapter, I list some key insights and takeaways that I have gleaned from the interviews. But don't feel compelled to rely on my conclusions alone. I encourage you to read the interviews and note what insights resonate with you. Which of these strategies can you adapt for your own purposes? Along with the entrepreneurs' strategies, I have added mental exercises—brain hacks, if you will—to develop your entrepreneur's mindset. Just as an athlete participates in rigorous physical training to be physically strong, so, too, must you engage in *mental* training in order to overcome challenges, stay on track, and succeed.

Before wrapping up, let me acknowledge the many brilliant people who have provided me with the theoretical basis for these interviews. In designing and framing the discussions contained herein, I relied upon these leaders' research in positive and social psychology. I have listed their names and books as additional resources at the end of the book.

On a further note, I want to thank the entrepreneurs I interviewed for sharing their stories and giving me more insight into the workings of an entrepreneur's mind. I have listed their names and positions at the time of their interviews. As is to be expected, with entrepreneurs often taking on new challenges, some have moved on. And so, I have noted their current positions in an addendum at the end of the book.

My greatest wish is for this book and these interviews to inspire you to be true to yourself, courageously pursue your passions, follow your dreams, and achieve your most incredible goals.

What Would Superman Do?

DUNCAN LOGAN

Founder and CEO of RocketSpace

RocketSpace – a tech community that helps tech start-ups grow

Lalia: Ashton Kutcher looks for grit in entrepreneurs for investment, and, so, [I'm looking at] what makes up that grit. Not only that but also how you can develop more of it in yourself. There's a lot of psychological research on what—I think—are the different components of grit, and there are ways to bootstrap your mind. I'm interviewing people just about their own entrepreneurial experience, but you have a broader picture, I think, because you know so many entrepreneurs.

Duncan: It's just observations that I hear about or see in other people. I kind of steal them with pride, if you like. There are some commonalities in what makes them [entrepreneurs] super good, which I try to take note of. I spend a lot of hours in the day learning about that. And then I've had businesses that failed, so I know what that feels like.

Lalia: I've been digging into the research, and they're having a hard time pinning down what an "entrepreneur" is. People have incredible experience and insight into things. Just because it hasn't been proven in a psychological test doesn't mean that it's wrong. On the other hand, there are some myths, I think, and one of them is that entrepreneurs are creative, happy people who are intrinsically and inherently driven from birth. That's not true. I've seen fearful people who have developed into what they need to be. A little bit of a myth is that they start that way—some do; some start with a lemonade stand—but not all.

Duncan: There are proven breakers to every rule.

Lalia: There is quite a lot of depression and even suicide among entrepreneurs, and that's not obvious or evident. That means that people are not resilient, not resistant to failure, don't have the coping skills to get back up and keep going.

Duncan: I think that's a good starting point because being able to control that emotion is super hard but also super important. In a funny sort of way, drugs or alcohol are fascinating in that sense. If you have a big night out or take a drug, it alters your thinking state. You're thinking, "Wow, here I was an hour ago down in the dumps, and now I am out with my friends and had a few drinks. The world couldn't be rosier." But you also know tomorrow [you're] probably going to feel like hell in the world, and then you realize that your brain or your mind is this chemical set of unbalances, and it's easily affected. When you bring that [understanding] into business, and you get some bad news, and you feel that the world is going to end, [you can say], "Whoa, wait a minute—this is just a chemical reaction, and it will change. It will pass, and I can change it, and I can pass it."

I think there are times when [you're] running your business that you're thinking, "Oh, my God. This could all fall apart," and "How am I going to get up in the morning?" and "How am I going to face my family and friends or my wife or whatever?" That's what you feel, and then you go back to that experience and think, *But that's just a feeling; it's not reality.*

Lalia: Your mental strategies as an entrepreneur that keep you going are fascinating. I love what you're saying because it's about self-leadership. It is about you. It's the knowing that it is just a chemical, and it changes.

Duncan: The highs never last as long as you want them to. The lows never last as long as you expect them to. We were five years old, and I think we had a great first year, a strong second year; our third and fourth years were just hard work; it just felt as though we never got a break—we got three or four things that kind of went against us. This is the part that separates the entrepreneur. I think if I hadn't been there, saying, "You guys can all pack up and leave. I'm going to keep going. The market is coming toward us; this will get better," it would have ended.

Lalia: What do you think goes on in your brain that gets you back on track, that keeps saying, "I'm going to keep going"?

Duncan: There's a critical assessment I think you have to do—the process of thinking you go through to say why you think it's going to get better, because the opposite is horrible as well. Before I had

RocketSpace, I had another company that never got off the ground. When I finally shut it down after two years and a ton of money, I looked at my thought process, and I should have shut it down a year earlier, but I couldn't bring myself to [do] it. You know, everything is part of the experience, but the assessment of that was: I was kidding myself that things were going to get better without some enormous change in strategy. I hate the "pivot into a new vision," but that was what it needed. With RocketSpace, when we were getting into tough times, when we were losing money, we could easily sort that out. There are tough decisions you can make. When your manager says, "I can't do it with less than a team of three," you say, "Show me what you can do with one, because that's all you're going to have," and you do that across all the divisions until you get profitable. I look at these major corporations that go bust, and I think, Is it ridiculous? They had sales of $3 billion, but they couldn't make the tough decisions to get their cost under the value of the sale.

Lalia: You had a self-confidence that, with this, you could make it.

Duncan: Right. I want RocketSpace to be hundreds of millions of dollars. I think that's the opportunity. You know, hundreds of millions of dollars in revenue, hundreds of millions if not billions of dollars in value. That's where I want it to be. Where we were stuck was kind of, I don't know—five, six million dollars in revenue and maybe twenty billion dollars in value. Now the crazy thing about that is here in the Valley, that seems like a disaster. If you sell a company here for five million dollars, people here say, "Oh, okay. I hope you didn't waste more than a year on that sort of thing. *Now* what are you going to do?" Harsh, so I think you have to bring that into context.

Lalia: Is there a personal trait that you would like to have more of in your business success?

Duncan: Where do I start? I have worked for not-so-nice guys who are phenomenal leaders. I would rather be the latter than the former, to be honest, because of the quality of your life. So, I think, unfortunately, I am more of the former.

Lalia: You're a nice guy.

Duncan: Too nice a guy, but when you're working for someone meticulous, consistent, focused, and then very quickly, the whole organization comes in behind him, and he's very consistent with what he says.

We brought that CEO into the company beforehand. We were 900 people. Everyone was frantically busy; everyone said, "I need more team; I need more people." Working till late at night, early in the morning, and working weekends. Then we brought in this professional CEO to take us public, and he said, "Guys, we're doing far too many things. These are the five things we're going to focus on. So, we're going to let 200 people go." Then we suddenly became profitable. He'd say, "Focus on this," and suddenly you start seeing that the car park starts emptying by seven o'clock at night. Progress starts going faster and faster, and there is discipline. Having a disciplined approach to work is a far nicer way to work. That's why I constantly strive to get there.

Lalia: That's great. Let me flip the question. What do you think are your strengths as an entrepreneur?

Duncan: It's a strength when it works, but it can also be a weakness. I think it takes an entrepreneur to look at a situation and say, "Here's the opportunity." It takes an entrepreneur to sit in a meeting, hear what all the people are saying, and listen to what they're saying. When other people would say, "Well, it doesn't look like you want to buy our service," I think an entrepreneur says, "If I understand what you're trying to get, and we did this and this, would that help?" And they say, "Yeah, that would be great."

An entrepreneur needs—and I have that ability—to sit with people and weed out the opportunity, the ability to sit with people—investors and so forth—and get across what our story is. Whereas, if you had other people in the organization do that, it probably wouldn't come to much.

You know, somebody said, to be great at sales, sales is just transferred enthusiasm from one person to another, and I believe that. I think that your enthusiasm as an entrepreneur has to be infectious. Every day you come into the office, [your attitude] has got to be, "This is the best day here." Because you're selling to your team every time you walk past a team member, every time you walk into the reception [area]. Every time you're selling, you're very happy.

Also, I think having a positive attitude no matter [what] is going on in the background. You think, "I can do nothing on that until my meeting at four o'clock this afternoon." So, until then, everything else is rosy. Just because we have that problem, it doesn't mean everything in here isn't rosy.

Lalia: You have the capability of shutting out and focusing on what's happening right now and dealing with what you have to deal with.

Duncan: It's knowing that very, very few things in the world are final or fatal. There have probably been a dozen times when someone has come up to me and said, "We're f**cked. They're pressing charges. We're done. We need the money. They're not going to pay. They've canceled the order. We're not going to get the deal." You're sitting there, looking at the numbers and thinking, "Okay. As it stands today, on Wednesday, we cannot pay payroll on Friday. We're trading insolvently."

When everyone else would pull the ripcord, you go and have a coffee, and you think, "What would Superman do here?" That sort of thing. I love the whole "Something will come to mind." Every time I've done that, something has, and we've survived.

I sold my first company, which was great. The company I shut down was a total decision of mine. We'd been offered investor money, we'd been offered stuff, and I said, "Actually, even if I took your money, I don't, in my heart, know how I would turn this into a really viable business. So, I'm going to shut it down."

Lalia: There's a time to fold up, and that doesn't mean that you're not an optimist or you don't have the grit or whatever. It's just really assessing things.

Duncan: Assessing your scope. The biggest thing with the previous company was, fundamentally, it was a technology company. It was a piece of technology that we were going to build, and I am not a techie, so I'm constantly asking, "Can we do this with the technology? Well, could we do this, or could we do that? (How) much will that be?" When you are taking this secondhand information, and the person you're asking, unless they're some genius co-founder—and that wasn't my case—they'd say, "It will do this." Then two weeks later, I'd ask, "Is it going to do that? Oh, yes. I see how you mean it could do that." I was just always on the back foot. It came to a point where I thought that I needed to learn to code, and I needed three months off—[either] that [or] this is just not the business for me.

Lalia: There are the entrepreneurs who know their strengths and know their weaknesses, and if they have an area of weakness, they can fill it with a co-founder or whomever. But they know that; they understand it instead of not being aware.

Duncan: I think that's something I'm very conscious of. Companies are better when there's a diversity of thought in the process, in the leadership team. On our executive team, some people are more similar to me; they're either glass-half-full or very "Boom! Let's go for it." Then we have the glass-half-empty crew: "But what happens if it doesn't happen and we don't have a government cover?" The truth is they're brilliant because they're going to stop me from running this thing off the cliff, when *I* think everything is going great. There will be times—thank God—we won't go quite as big and bold and brash. That's the thing: You don't build a company— you build a team.

Lalia: When there's too much groupthink, that is a bad thing. You have to have the other perspective. You're running right into my next set of questions, which is about optimism, because I think you described yourself as an optimist.

Duncan: Yeah, I think optimism is super important. I think it will be very hard, as a pessimist, to run a business. You know, it's the difference: Are you fearful of failure or driven by success? I think there are founders in both. I'm definitely driven by success. I rarely, rarely think of failure, and I always back myself. If I had ten dollars to my name, sitting on the street on Monday the 1st of

January, by twelve months forward, I'd be fine as long as I have my mental stability. I'd probably be where I am now, so I have no problem backing my abilities.

Lalia: Describe a positive event that's happened in starting this business or any business, and what part did you have to play? So, let me explain. One psychological study compared MBA students who said they would be entrepreneurs to those planning to become managers. The future entrepreneurs rated highly in the "proactive" personality, and it's very similar to optimism, where they think, "I take charge of my environment. If something bad happens, it's just the circumstances. It's not permanent. It's not my fault." It's that sense that "I played a part in this, making this thing happen."

Duncan: I have this. What you're bringing up is something that I'm a fundamental believer in, which is the five on the dice. So, the thesis of RocketSpace for these young companies, young people—is that you are a product of your environment. And you should take that really, really seriously. When I was in university, a person said to me, "You take your four best friends and put yourself in the middle, and you will be the average of them." The four people you hang out with, who influence you, what their relationships are like, what their happiness is like, what their sporting achievements are like—you will be pretty much the average of them.

I looked at that—and at my four best friends—and guess what? It's scary how true that is. I went to Aberdeen University—that's where we all were—and we all played First XV rugby. We all had a really small amount of money because we would be doing evening jobs. We were prepared to get our butts up to work in a bar or open the door or whatever, but it was kind of scary. Then we all moved to London, and guess what? We all ended up in banking, and we all ended up earning good wages in London, and life moved on.

Because your friends, by definition, are average. So, your friends' advice is kind of average. It takes an enormous amount of effort to pull yourself out of average, to get up into elite status of whatever you want to do. Part of that is you have to pack your bags. If you're going to be a ballerina, you can sit in San Francisco and be a pretty average ballerina, or you can realize that, actually, the two best schools for ballet are in Paris and Moscow.

After twelve years in London of denial-visit here and denial-visit there, I said, "Okay. I know this exists here, so why don't I change?" I told my friends, "Guys, I'm off to San Francisco." They were saying, "What are you doing there? Don't be stupid. You have friends here." I said, "I am off to San Francisco because I want to build a tech company; that's where the best tech companies are built, and I want to start. I just want to immerse myself in it." I got here, and I started. My first company failed. They were all saying, "Okay. Have you got that out of your system? Come back, welcome." And I'm saying, "No—I'm just getting started." RocketSpace is now a couple hundred million. It might get to the b-word or whatever. But the reason is that the caliber of people I hang out with here is different. I think this location in the world has a lot of above-average people going throughout.

Lalia: What do you feel your locus of control is in the midst of a negative event that's happened to you?

Duncan: Humans are amazing with what they can survive. I have a one-year-old boy. He kind of changes bits of the way you see the world. I look at these refugees in Europe, who have walked with toddlers and babies without food, cover, or shelter. They got on a boat in North Africa; they'd risk floating across the ocean for four days without food, without water. They get found in Greece. They get up, get some food, walk another six days to get into Germany, and get there. They're just average people, really determined to stay alive.

If you are told that you're going to be sued, or it's the worst news you've had to wake up to, then pull yourself together. It's amazing what we can do in really horrendous situations—that 99% percent of us will never find ourselves in, ever—so, when businesses go wrong, bring it into proportion. It's just a bad [time], not a bad life.

I go into the big picture of things. Will this matter in a year? Really? So, someone says they are leaving. "No, you're such a good person and critical. In a year, I don't think we'll survive…" Of course, we will survive. Then, in a year, we will be thriving even more so.

Lalia: That's a coaching question that's used often: "What's the worst thing that can happen here, just for the sake of the exercise?" Somebody says, "Oh, my God. If I were out on the street, I could survive." It's basically not becoming a victim to it.

Duncan: You talk about suicide and the suicide rate. I got divorced, and my business went bust; I thought, "So?" Tough time? Sure. In the world? Absolutely not. You haven't been anywhere near to what the worst situation in the world is, where those people don't quit. They get on a boat; they say they will reset the clock in some other place.

Lalia: People have hard lives, and you bring it into context. So, what do you personally think about risk?

Duncan: We see this with the big corporations we deal with. You go through the sign-off processes and all the different people who have to put their stamp on a piece of paper for a million-dollar, or two-million-dollar, or forty-million-dollar purchase. You realize very quickly that a lot of people in big corporations—the vast majority of people in big corporations—will not make a decision without data. They want to know how do you know you're going somewhere? How do you know you're going to do this? How do you know you're going to do that?' When are you going to deliver on this? And they want proof that you can, and they want everything, with all the data, so that they can make their decision.

Entrepreneurs deal with no data, you know. We don't have a clue. What's the sales forecast for next year? I really don't know. You deal in the unknown. You become very comfortable in lack of certainty. My wife asks, "When are going to know that we can do this again?" I don't know. We want to move to Santa Barbara, so she was already asking, "So when are we going to move to Santa Barbara?" I said, "I don't know yet—couple of years." She says, "How do you mean, 'a couple of years'?" I replied, "I can tell you the conditions that need to exist here for us to go and do that. When we get there, we'll get there." I think entrepreneurs kind of get very comfortable, very quickly, with doing the unknown.

Lalia: How do you view goal-setting?

Duncan: It's changed a little bit on my personal view, because I think I was far too goal-driven. In the sense of, "I want to do this, and I want to achieve that, and be totally focused on that." Everything was about the destination; nothing was about the journey, and I think maybe it's an age thing, but I think [it's] far more about the journey. We could try to get to here next year and just break it—you know, break ourselves—to do that. Or we could say, "Actually, here is still super successful, slightly more enjoyable." I'm still very goal-oriented. I'm not totally religious about [it], you know—[I'm] not the guy who gets up saying into the mirror, "Okay, here's the four things I'm going to achieve." But I definitely write down goals of where I want to get to. I think it's a healthy thing. In the company, we're doing things called OKR—objectives and key results. [We do them] on a quarterly basis to focus the company this quarter. That's what's important and what we all agreed on—that sort of thing.

Lalia: Many entrepreneurs start without understanding that you've got to start leadership from the beginning. It is the people, the team.

Duncan: I say this to students all the time: "You're the entrepreneur, but, trust me—you're going to have very little to do in running your business. All you have to focus on is building that team and running the team. They'd better be passionate in your vision—only then can they deliver."

■ ■ ■ ■ ■

Key Strategies: Duncan Logan

KEEP YOUR EYE ON THE BIGGER PICTURE
In times of struggle and strife, Duncan tries to take a macro view of the situation. He asks himself questions like, "Will this problem really matter in a few months?" Or "When compared to more significant real-world problems, genuine tragedies, is my situation really so grim?" You may recognize this principle—it's a common

one called "psychological distancing." In Duncan's case, he uses it to replenish his store of optimism regularly. Recall his missive that "Very, very few things in the world are final or fatal." By maintaining such a clear-eyed perspective on the broader picture, he's able to remain positive through the ups and downs of a business venture.

ALWAYS LOOK FOR THE OPPORTUNITY

To Duncan's thinking, an entrepreneur must be ready to glimpse the opportunity lying hidden within any situation. Whether it's a client or an investor—or maybe even an employee—who notices a problem with his product or service, Duncan doesn't lay blame or stew over the issue. Instead, he draws out their key objection, re-communicates the "story" of the business, and works toward a solution that might strengthen the overall enterprise.

ELEVATE YOUR SOCIAL NETWORK

Few of us would ever have the courage to move halfway across the world, but Duncan did precisely that. Why? So he could surround himself with successful players in the start-up world. As Duncan pointed out with his "Five on the Dice" concept, we are each the average of any five people around us in life. Indeed, studies have shown that an individual's social network frequently affects their level of success in career, family life, even health. That's also the principle behind RocketSpace itself—to create opportunities for start-up founders to surround themselves with other like-minded entrepreneurs. In many ways, by leaving Scotland and immersing himself amidst peers who challenged and elevated him, Duncan represents his own best proof of concept.

HOLD FAST TO YOUR ENTHUSIASM

According to Duncan, sales entails transferring enthusiasm to others. For him, the enthusiasm is not about selling a specific product or service but rather selling that positivity *itself*. In other words, the contagious quality of spirit sits at the core of his value proposition. As such, when he goes into the office with an attitude of "This is the best day here," his employees, as well as customers, are more likely to believe it.

PUT YOURSELF IN THE SHOES OF AN EXPERT

While most people don't think of Superman as a super-entrepreneur, Duncan invokes that character as a way of jarring himself out of his thoughts and behaviors, his limited sense of his abilities. By picturing himself as a Superman figure, he can better envision how to save the day. It's a well-known technique for creativity and problem-solving where you start thinking like someone else who is smarter, savvier, or more talented. The technique pushed him into a new mode of "out of the box" thinking for Duncan. The result? He *did* generate solutions to an array of challenging problems.

MINDSET EXERCISES

SEE THE BIGGER PICTURE

To get perspective when the going gets tough.

- Create a picture frame in your mind of a difficult circumstance you are currently experiencing, and put yourself in the center.
- What is happening to others around you in that picture?
- How are you doing in comparison to others?
- Increase the size of the picture to include a broader environment. How do your circumstances compare to those of others around you?
- Progressively increase the size of the frame to fit a picture of a broader and broader environment.

- Keep increasing the picture until you see the reality of how well you are doing.

- Even if some things are difficult, take time to appreciate how lucky you are with what you *do* have.

- How does showing empathy for others who are worse off affect you?

- Is there any action that you can take to help those less fortunate?

WHAT'S THE WORST THAT CAN HAPPEN?

This exercise is often used in coaching and counseling to help clients discover that they have the strengths and resources to manage and survive even the worst-case circumstances.

- Picture or describe an issue or problem that creates an undue amount of stress.

- What are your worst fears of what can happen?

- Expand on those fears to the worst-possible scenario (short of annihilation).

- What are some of the ways that you would handle the worst-case situation?

- What solutions could you use to manage it?

- Are there steps you could take to prevent the worst-case scenario from happening?

- What strengths do you have that could help address this situation?

FIND A ROLE MODEL

Self-efficacy, the belief in your ability to succeed, can be developed by observing and adopting the best characteristics of a role model.

- Conjure an image of an imaginary or real-life hero or role model you admire for their success.

- What are their characteristics that you admire?

- What can you do to adopt more of these characteristics?

- If these role models were to advise you on how to succeed, what would they tell you?

- Put yourself in one of these role models' mindset, and ask yourself, "What would they do when confronted with a situation or problem?"

The Obstacle Is Always the Way

LISA FETTERMAN

Founder and CEO of Nomiku

Nomiku—sous vide immersion circulators for home cooks

Lalia: You have a fantastic story about persistence, grit, resilience, and all of that. I wanted to hear more about that.

Lisa: Every present moment of my life, I am the best Lisa I have ever been. You are talking to the best Lisa ever. I have never been this good, and it is my best. I go after problems that way. First: What do I need to do to solve this problem? I know that, regardless of any problem, I can handle it because I am the best Lisa ever.

Lalia: You have a certain self-confidence. Where do you think that comes from?

Lisa: I think that a lot of it is that I am very risk tolerant. I fear things, but I know that it is going to be all right and that I really have very little control. If I hold myself accountable to something, and other people are watching, I will most likely perform. The more pressure there is on me, the better I perform.

Lalia: So, you feel you have control over your environment?

Lisa: I don't feel that I have control over the environment. But what I do feel is that I will be able to handle it regardless of what it is because I have my brain. I have more than what I need.

Lalia: Have you ever had moments of doubt in the process of doing this?

Lisa: Absolutely doubts. Every day, I have fresh doubts. But every day, I know that I have the confidence to do this. Also, I have maybe more grace, something a little bit more spiritual, to battle against this. I am a devout Christian. As Steve Jobs said: "You have to have something." There is a verse in the Bible where they talk about basics. They say, "Don't worry about tomorrow because today has enough of its own troubles." My biggest hurdle is controlling my emotions and my reactions so that I can face things.

Lalia: Did you ever feel like giving up?

Lisa: Of course, I feel like giving up when I am too tired or really sick: I had pneumonia two weeks ago. I had my first baby. I get overwhelmed all the time. I have a two-year-old.

I often have a failure fantasy. Like, *What happens if I just give up?* What's the worst that can happen? If I think about that, it's not so bad. Usually, I never really want to quit. If I ever say that I want to quit, it is really hypothetical: "What happens if I quit?" But then if I haven't quit, then, "What happens if I win? Yay! So, let's try that first." Quitting is easy. I can do it any time I want. Nothing is stopping me. But I am not going to, because I want to do it, because this is fun. I give myself the option. "Lisa, you can quit any time you want. You own you."

If I never let myself think about it, then I would be even more drawn to it. Because I know what it looks like. If I wanted to, I could.

Lalia: When there are challenges—you had challenges when you couldn't raise enough money, and you were going to sell a kidney—do you get depressed?

Lisa: I get sad. It does happen because you have to deal with everything. I allow myself to mourn if something bad happens. I know that it is shaping me to be better. Everything that I do that is good never, ever disappears. It builds me as a person, and I just get "gooder and gooder." Everything I do for good is not for naught. If I am suffering now, if I get depressed, it teaches me some kind of lesson. I may not know the lesson now; I know I have to go through it. I tell myself, "I have to go through this." It is never going to stop: If you get flipped over by this now, what about the next time?

One time we were making Nomiku Classic. Our factory stopped paying attention to us because we were one of their smaller clients. That made me sad. They took workers off our line. They were constantly delayed, which feels like the worst, but the worst that they could possibly do is ship a bad product. So, then I started paying more attention. We lived next to the factory in China. We went to the line ourselves; we taught ourselves manufacturing, which is how we were able to bring manufacturing here.

The thing with start-ups is that you expect to move fast, but some lessons that you learn grow you personally and the company—they may take a long time. It takes a long time to pull it together sometimes. That is the antithesis of what it takes as a fast-moving start-up, but I am getting more the hang of it now. It is an intense curve, especially if you have early success.

Lalia: Some people never make it as a success, as a CEO.

Lisa: That sucks. I would never want that to happen to me. I could never not be the CEO.

Lalia: Interesting numbers on that. More than 50% of founders are out by year three or four—unbelievably high.

Lisa: Nobody on planet Earth will care about this as much as me. I know that nobody will care about it as much as I do. I know more about this company than anybody—its future, present, and past.

Lalia: I think your future is solid, from my experience. What are your personal strengths that are useful for being a founder?

Lisa: Public speaking—I am very good at that. I double down whenever I do it. I learned how to be good through drama club—anything that I can do to get in front of people. It is only because I love it. It was a natural inclination, but I did have to build it. I just have to do it over and over.

It's important that I communicate fully with my team to make sure we are on the same page. When there is a new initiative and [we're] figuring something out together, I make sure that everyone is talking to each other and not so heads-down. So we have the same message and don't clash in our messaging.

Lalia: Do you have the people around you that complement your weaknesses?

Lisa: My co-founder, Abe, has a Ph.D. in plasma physics from Princeton. We are like Penn and Teller. He is the one that doesn't talk. He does all the tech. We don't compete on anything. What I lack on the technical side, the more analytical side—well, Abe will always say "No" to everything. He is the cynical one. I am the super-yes person. I say, "Oh, that is so good. Let's at least try it." But eventually, it adds up to a lot of your time. And Abe will say "No." We need a "No" person. If I can convince him, I can convince everybody. We are very complementary.

Lalia: Do you see yourself using your strengths to manage your weaknesses?

Lisa: No, my weaknesses are weak, and I keep them weak. I am not looking to make my weaknesses any better. If I do that, I will be mediocre by taking time away from my strengths and superstrengths. Everything that I am good at, I double down, triple down. Anything that I am not good at, I hire someone for that.

Lalia: Do you think you are an optimist?

Lisa: I am a super optimist. Glass half-full. I feel happy when I am sad. I feel happy, a divine joy. People say that I am an optimist, even if I am sad. I don't know how it is possible, but I feel happy in my deepest, darkest sadness. Kind of a divine, joyful thing.

My mom got breast cancer, and I got really depressed and sad. I felt so low that I vomited. I felt so sick, and, after that, I was really happy that I could feel that way. I really love my mom *and* that I can experience life and experience a bad thing, and I am taking it. That's how I know I am an optimist.

Lalia: Is there a negative experience that you have had in this business?

Lisa: I feel like there is no separation [between] personal and business. This is just my life. I feel like my personal experiences directly affect my business experiences. If you are going to invest in me, as an investor or as an employee, you have to know everything. You have to know that I will fight for this, but it has to be with my entire life.

Lalia: Flip side, what are some positive things that have happened?

Lisa: We joined Y-Combinator; I got on Forbes 30 under 30; we sold thousands of units used by every top chef in the world. I can list them for days and days. Lunch was delicious.

Lalia: What part did you play in these things?

Lisa: All the parts, at least one part of it. I am the leader—every good part, I take credit for; every bad part, I take credit for. If it is a delay, it is my fault. If we run out of money, it is my fault. Someone is not getting along with somebody at the company, that is my fault for not communicating with them better. Everything bad that happens is my fault. Everything great that happens, I had a part in it with my team. But everything catastrophic that happens rests on just one person, and that's me.

Lalia: Is it your fault or responsibility? So, if there is an earthquake and this building falls, is that your fault?

Lisa: Legally, no. In my heart, I would feel responsible. I would feel really bad: "Oh, I should have earthquake-proofed this. I should not have had it in San Francisco." I would feel bad about it on a personal level.

Lalia: What would be your next steps?

Lisa: My next steps [would be] to look ahead to see what the world looks like now, now that it has happened.

Lalia: Would you take it personally, in the sense that this kind of thing always happens to you?

Lisa: No, I am a survivor, not a victim. Good things always happen. I am super lucky. Bad things do not always happen. They can happen, and it is a lesson; and also, when bad things happen to me, I could feel that they are bad. But my understanding of it is that they are not real. Good things are always good, but bad things, you just don't know, because your definition of bad is so not real, you can't trust that understanding about bad things.

Lalia: Do you want people to say you are smart or getting better?

Lisa: Yes, I do want them to say I am smart, but here's the thing: In terms of Maslow's hierarchy of needs, if you have self-actualization, all the recognition will come. It feels so good. I love having a great reputation, and I work really hard at it. I help entrepreneurs. I kept a lot of things open-source. My reputation is really important. I want to look very good, and at the same time, I want to improve myself. They are both really important.

Lalia: You seem like a perpetual learner. How do you think that helps?

Lisa: Ooh, definitely. That's like the thing every religion says: You have to learn your whole life. The Sikh religion talks about learning; the Torah says you have to learn your whole life. Every single day. And those are enduring stories that have carried on for years and years. What does it mean? We are trying to tell you to be a learner, and so I definitely dedicate myself to that.

Lalia: Tell me about goals.

Lisa: I love goals! My goals are to grow my company a lot, and my goals are to make everyone in the world know *sous vide* cooking. Also, to keep my employees forever—I never want anyone to leave. And a really meaningful and purposeful life, where I feel like I contribute to the world.

Super, super goal—immortal status, like Steve Jobs or Oscar Wilde.

Lalia: Do you have any goal-setting strategies? For example, some people write things down every day.

Lisa: I do have task lists every day. All my goals are very high level. I do have tasks to fulfill, but my big goals are really big, so I never reach them. I know supposedly to be happy is to set goals that you reach. But I never really do that. My big goals are always reaching higher and higher, and I find that motivating.

Lalia: Do you take into account the obstacles when reaching your goals?

Lisa: I never take the obstacles into account. Not for the big goals. For a task, yes. Like, you have to ship now—that's a task. I plan very meticulously.

Lalia: When there is an obstacle, do you look at alternative ways?

Lisa: The obstacle is always the way. Every time I have had an obstacle, it is a part of the solution. You have to consider that when you want to move the obstacle out of the way. This rock is part of the story. I need to know why it is. So, I look at the rock, and I say, "What is it doing now, and why is it here now? What can I do about it? What part of the solution is the rock?"

For example, manufacturing has a lot of roadblocks. In each roadblock, I say, "Okay, this is part of the solution, and then we have to work with it." Like, when you can't get the right color in a plastic part, what is the roadblock to causing that color to work? That is part of the solution. So, I have everyone huddle around it. We are not moving away; we are going to stare at it. We are going to figure out how to get there—maybe adding another material.

Lalia: What is the most important personal factor that contributes to your success?

Lisa: Risk acceptance and being a happy person.

■ ■ ■ ■ ■

Key Strategies: Lisa Fetterman

QUITTING IS ALWAYS AN OPTION

Lisa prefers to lower the pressure on herself by sometimes engaging in a failure fantasy. "You can always throw in the towel and walk away," she might tell herself. Does it sound counterintuitive, the notion that an entrepreneur might find comfort and calm by envisioning the worst-case scenario? Well, that's because it is. And yet, the whole exercise serves as a reminder that her life isn't hanging in the balance. It's only a business, after all. From there, she's able to reframe the scenario. "Sure, quitting is one option, but wouldn't it taste a whole lot sweeter to *win*?" she might coach herself. And by looking at the equation from both sides, she re-empowers herself. She's in the driver's seat. The choice is hers to make, and she chooses to win. Knowing Lisa, even when the time comes to quit, she will spin it into a victory.

DOUBLE DOWN ON YOUR STRENGTHS

You might spot a recurring theme in many of these dialogues. Nearly all of my interview subjects held fast to an awareness of their strengths and weaknesses. Few of them placed much value in the notion of improving on their shortcomings unless it was a learning opportunity. After all, why squander time and energy working to rectify a weakness? It's far from your best use of time—imagine an Olympic sprinter deciding they wanted to brush up on their swimming skills. Such is the case with Lisa. She "doubles-down" on her strengths by nurturing and honing them further. For her, fine-tuning her weak spots will only—at best—bring her to the level of average. It would merely land her in the middle of the pack. Lisa, much like that Olympic sprinter, prefers to get out ahead of her competitors.

THE OBSTACLE *IS* THE WAY

Essential to Lisa's outstanding perseverance is her ability to reframe her thinking, re-characterize obstacles, and give them a positive connotation. She starts by understanding the obstacle itself—the "rock," as she calls it. If she can understand why an impediment has landed in her path, she can grasp what is needed to overcome it. The process yields creative solutions that might not have otherwise appeared. It also endows Lisa with a remarkable tolerance for risk. So long as she reminds herself that every problem carries the seeds of its own solution, she can discover that solution for herself. Such a mindset provides her with the confidence vital to confronting challenges.

BE A SUPER-HAPPY OPTIMIST

Most of the entrepreneurs interviewed for this book confirmed themselves as inveterate optimists. No huge surprise there, right? That said, each of them placed their unique spin on that optimism. Lisa, for her part, believes that personal happiness is one of the most important contributors to her success as an entrepreneur. Her happiness is not a goofy sort; it's not the kind of happiness that refuses to acknowledge or confront sadness. Relying upon her strong spiritual anchor, she readily allows herself to experience darker tones of emotion, and yet she can rest assured that happiness awaits her on the other side, tasting all the sweeter after the bitter herbs of struggle.

SET SUPER-GOALS FOR YOURSELF

For Lisa, achievement is a process without an end. No matter how high she has climbed, there always remains another, higher pinnacle. She always knows she will keep pushing bigger and further. Her super-goals are numerous, too: She wants to expand her business to the point where everyone uses the product, her employees lead better lives, and the wider world benefits. That said, while her super-goals are vast, she prefers to deal in concrete, specific, manageable details, always relying on task lists and meticulous modes of planning.

MINDSET EXERCISES

BEST SELF

For when you need to understand your strengths, what you are good at, and leverage them for better performance. Describe three to five of the top strengths that you have identified for yourself.

- Think of a time when you used one of your top strengths

- Compile a list of five people who know you well either personally or professionally. Ask them for feedback on what they think are your best strengths.

- When you receive your feedback, collect and analyze them for common themes.

- What resonated with you? What surprised you?

- Look for examples of when you have used those strengths. What was the impact of focusing on them?

- Which of your strengths can become weaknesses when they are overused?

- Carefully assess your weaknesses. Are any of them potentially undeveloped strengths?

- Which of your weaknesses is a waste of time to focus on?

- How can you find someone else in your business to offset those weaknesses?

- How can you build on these strengths and use them for better performance?

- Check out some of the Strengths Tests offered online to help you discover your hidden strengths. (See Resources)

FROM OBSTACLE TO OPPORTUNITY

Turn your fears and worries into opportunities.

- What are some of the current obstacles and problems that you are facing in your business?

- What do you need to gain the confidence that you can overcome the challenges?

- How have you dealt with a significant obstacle in the past?

- How did you come up with a solution to the problem?

- How did you turn that past problem into an opportunity?

- How did you manage your own mindset to keep going?

- How might your current problem be an opportunity "in disguise"?

- What resources do you need to solve the problem?

- What resources do you need to turn this into an opportunity?

- What are the next steps you need to take?

IT'S YOUR CHOICE

When quitting might be the right option.

Imagine the scenario of quitting, giving up, or closing down your business.

- In this scenario, what are you doing? What are you thinking? How are you feeling? How is your body experiencing this?

- Bring up the alternative picture in your mind—the one where you have stuck it out. What are you thinking? How are you feeling? How is your body experiencing this?

- In your "quitting" scenario, what would make it a successful outcome?

- What if you don't quit? How might *that* be a failure?

- Pros and cons lists: Make two lists with the pros and cons for both situations.

- Armed with the two ways of looking at the choice—subjectively and objectively—what do you conclude is the right choice?
- What more information might you need to make the right decision?
- Reiterate this process as many times as you need to.

Failures Are Success Learnings

GUY PRAISLER

Founder and CEO of Dine Market

Dine Market—a wholesale marketplace where restaurateurs can connect with local suppliers for anything they might need

Lalia: Thank you for talking with me today. I know you're really busy, so let's get started. Is Dine Market your first venture?

Guy: No, this is my fourth one. I started doing my first one in '98, and it was an online e-commerce store, at the time when the whole e-commerce thing was just really starting on the internet.

Lalia: So you're a serial entrepreneur.

Guy: Yes, I am—with everything that comes with it.

Lalia: And everything that comes with it—we're going to get to that. Did you consider those businesses to be successes? Failures? How did you do in your previous ventures?

Guy: My previous businesses were all self-financed, organically grown, and they were a success. It was a success for me, for my customers—they were all sold—even for my employees there, also. But we didn't completely get to the true potential of the businesses. That's what made me go after investors' money this time. So we can be a lot more aggressive and create a much bigger business.

Lalia: When you experienced a difficult time in either this business or the others, how did you overcome these, personally? How did you overcome some of the obstacles and the challenges?

Guy: The most important thing is to build a support system around you, and the most important support you can get is, first, from your immediate family. So, you need to be transparent with your family. You need to explain to them where you are right now. You don't need to show the details, but they need to understand where you are, and you actually can share with them what can help you. For example, right now, we're going through a demanding period; it's demanding a lot of time. I share with my wife, and I tell her: "The next six months, I'm not going to be able to do a lot of the things that I did before, and this is why, and this is where I need your help." So, certain things, I really don't want to miss. If I know them in advance, then I will be able to change my schedule to make sure I am not missing a lot of other things.

Then you have additional friends and family circles around you. Some of them are more as professionals; some of them are just for more emotional support. Then there is a third layer—the investors and other consultants who are less involved directly with your business, and sometimes it's easier for these people to see the bigger picture. You collect a lot of information, a lot of feedback, and then, at one point, you have enough. I guess when you feel that you have enough, you can sit down and make your decisions. I think that the most important thing is, from the very beginning, to really start creating this support system around you—different circles for different purposes.

Lalia: Have there ever been moments of doubt? When you felt like giving up?

Guy: Well, it's two things. You always have doubts. I mean—I'm sorry. You don't always have doubts, but you have a lot. It's a roller coaster. And every time you know that you're going downhill, you doubt everything. But this is kind of your protection. I guess it's going to protect you because it makes you see what does and what doesn't work. Do I need to change something? Is it something temporary, and I just need to ride the wave, or do I need to take drastic steps to make sure that—very quickly—I'm going to start going uphill as well? There's always those doubts, and I think it's important to understand it for what is and be very calculated during these times.

I think that the business opportunity was there, so the challenge was *how to make it work*. It's super-important to be in this state of mind, and if you see these doubts coming and you feel that you are getting weak—a friend of mine said that he does the same thing—you put on your sneakers, go out, run, go to the gym, take a good shower. Then you sit down in front of the computer and start putting everything together to understand what the challenge is and how you can turn it around.

I was lucky enough that I think the businesses I had—there were doubts, but there was no doubt that it could be turned into a successful business. You have your doubts, so what you need to do is get into your euphoria, and jogging does that great for me. You get into that euphoria, so now you're coming from a positive point in trying to solve your challenges.

Lalia: What do you find are your major stress points, the kinds of things that keep you up at night?

Guy: Financial aspects of the business are the biggest challenge. That's the lifeblood of any company, and managing it is super challenging. Sometimes you can see really interesting, very appealing opportunities, and you need to decide, "Do I take that on, and can it give me aggressive growth, customers, revenues? But then it's going to put me in a very little, very thin margin for a while before it's going to pick up. And what's going to happen if it's not going to pick up in the right [amount of] time?" You always should be mindful about it to make the best decision when it comes to budgeting.

Lalia: There is this talk about how good it is to fail and how important it is to embrace failure and all of that. What do you think about the concept of failing?

Guy: Failings? The road to success is built with and combined with a lot of failures. You have to borrow going up, but you have these slowdowns, which is actually failure. So, we call them "success learnings." If you did something, and, from the beginning, it was very successful—and I think we see it also with other entrepreneurs—you are not always going to be able to replicate it. There's not a lot of things that probably made you very successful in a very short time. There are actually very few of those.

When we fail, we are definitely learning from the process; we understand the process. We go over it again and again, making sure that we're not going to fail again in the same way or in a similar way. For me, if somebody doesn't fail a couple of times with more than one start-up, you have to look more into why it happened. You can learn a lot from that because you have never been there before. Failure is just part of the business; most of the start-up companies are failing.

I read somewhere that 95% of the technology start-ups that raised more than a million dollars have closed their doors. It means only 5% success. That's one out of twenty—that's a huge number. Most of them are failing. But a lot of them are trying again and again, and it's enough to be successful once, and it is enough to make it for you, your family, your employees, and your investors. I just see that failure is probably one of the best opportunities to learn.

Lalia: I know your businesses were ultimately a success. But within that, did you experience failure, and what did you learn?

Guy: I mean, we believe that it's very successful, so far. But to get to the point where it's a successful business [in the sense] that everybody, all the stockholders, have gotten returns from the success—well, we're not there yet. We have to work very hard for some time to get there. But a company pivots, and a lot of companies do that. That's because they did something that wasn't good enough. Or you can say that, in a way, its process failed, and we're changing it to trying a different process until we're going to figure out what the successful process for our business is.

Every success has a lot of failure points in its way. The most important [thing] is to realize that, if something doesn't work—the process is not good enough, the market is too small, the service is not a good fit for the market—whatever it is, the sooner you figure it out, the more opportunity you have to change it, fix it, learn from it, and come up with a much better product. It can be small failure or big failure. If the company just ends up closing, they might have had a great idea, and the market [just] wasn't ready for it. Now they learn how to evaluate the much better market opportunity in the future job.

Lalia: In terms of how you handle everything, what do you think your personal strengths are as an entrepreneur?

Guy: I think that my past experience doing different things in my career helped me take a step back and evaluate a different aspect of the business. *Always question everything.* Even if it seems to work okay, you still have to question it. If it works okay, then it can work better. I mean, what it allows you to do is to, very quickly, in the early stages, find different processes that maybe are not good enough and can grow into a problem. In the beginning, you want to solve these issues very quickly. I call them "cheap mistakes," and you've got to resolve them before they become a big, expensive one. At the same time, there's a lot of "how" decisions that you have to make. You have to be able to step back, evaluate them, and make these decisions very quickly. It's being able to react very quickly, evaluate things, and then make some judgments and react to them quickly. It has to be done very fast.

With every little thing you are doing, you are making decisions. Because of the speed at which these start-ups are growing, every small decision actually has a very big impact on the future of the company.

Lalia: So what do you think your weaknesses are?

Guy: My weaknesses... That is a good question. It's not that I don't know; I just don't know where to start. I don't know anyone who doesn't have them; the problem is when you *don't recognize* them. If you have a weakness, what you do is you hire amazing people who are going to do it so much better than you can. For example, I'm good at looking at something at the micro level. But I do need somebody to help me at the macro level. As we grow—and this is actually something that I saw [in] a couple of other entrepreneurs who had started some small businesses—you have your hands in every aspect of that business.

As the business grows, you have to start delegating and very much let go. I need to hire somebody I can trust enough to do what I would have done or even actually do what needs to be done *much better* than I would do it. That is part of my letting go. So, not to take ownership of every process in the company—that's a learning curve as well. It has to do with hiring the right people and, potentially, hiring somebody much smarter than you are. So how do you do that? And then to monitor and make sure that was actually the right person for the job. I guess this is what I'm going through.

I don't know, exactly, how to define my weaknesses, but I'm very persistent, in a way that I am stubborn. In a previous business that I had, a technology start-up, there was a point where many of my advisors told me that this was a good time to close and to move on. I refused to do that, and, at the end of the day, I was able to sell it, and it was a nice exit. But looking backward, knowing what I know now compared to then, they were probably right. If I had gotten out and then gotten into something else and used everything that I had learned, maybe I wouldn't have had to start from the bottom, and

I might have been able to create something much more successful and bigger. To know when to actually say, "Okay, this is not going to work—I admit that," takes a lot of courage.

Lalia: This is the first time I've heard somebody put it that way. Because I know entrepreneurs who refuse to give it up. They just keep going. It's clear that it's not going to succeed, and they do damage to their lives, their family's lives—I mean, literally.

Guy: Exactly. It takes a lot of courage to make this decision. You have to be a very strong person to go through the process. So, the reason you're not going to make this decision is being afraid of what comes up after. It's pretty much fear mixed with a scary imagination. We're afraid of something that hasn't happened yet. I found that, once you jump into the cold water, it's okay. Because, after that, you just keep swimming.

But for the first steps, it takes a lot of courage. When you are doing that, it's not what it's going to cost *you*. It's what it will cost the people *around* you—your family, maybe your friends, maybe your investors, whoever. What are you going to do if it doesn't work? So, you're a great entrepreneur. You know how to raise more money, and you *do* raise more money, but, in the end, it's still not going to work. Many people actually get hurt from it, or a lot of resources might be wasted because of not doing the right thing at the right time.

Lalia: That's excellent. Do you think you're an optimist?

Guy: Yes. I wouldn't be an entrepreneur if I were not an optimist. To start a new company, a start-up, pretty much what we are doing is we are trying to create a new product or service. A lot of the time, it's for a new market that doesn't yet exist. The reason that there's nothing like it out there is that, probably, nobody believed that it would work. When I started Dine Market, there were many people at the beginning—when I started bouncing around the idea—who told me it would never work. Most of the people from the industry told me that I was going to waste my time and my money for even trying. "It will never work." This is when you say, "Okay, this is actually an opportunity, because there are almost no competitors, because nobody believes it will work. And it's a tremendous market." All the fear around you is actually an opportunity.

You take that and say, "Okay, everybody thinks that it's going to fail. Let me do that—it will be super successful." You have to be onto something or be very optimistic to actually take the first step. After all of that, you have to really understand what you are up against and create the right story to start getting the support around you: the first employees you are hiring who believe this is a real opportunity, the first investor who believes that nobody was successful in this market until now because it wasn't started by somebody like you. I don't know how you cannot be an optimist as an entrepreneur.

Lalia: The definition of "optimism" used within this kind of psychology has more to do with a sense of self-confidence or, a better term might be *self-agency*—a sense that you have control. It's knowing that there's always something that you can do. There's always some sense that you have personal effectiveness, that you can take charge and be proactive around whatever the situation is, good or bad.

Guy: I mean, there's *always* an option. You might have five horrible options, but one of them is *less* horrible than the others, so there's *always* an option. This is actually your job: to make sure that you always have an option. Every time you get to a fork in the road, you have to evaluate not only which way you're going to go, but where it's going to lead and what you will need to do once you get there. And to make sure that, when you've taken this [path], it's an opening to other options. If you're going to take only one option, it's probably the wrong one to take.

If somebody says, "Well, you know, there's no other option," that means he's refused to evaluate the others. But there's really *always* something you can do about it; there's *always* more than one way.

Lalia: Describe, in the process of starting this business, a positive event that happened. What part did you personally play in this positive event coming about?

Guy: Most of my businesses were business-to-business. You're working with the other professionals, but you get to really touch them. The service that you're building is you get to see exactly how they need it, how they use it, what they're getting out of it, and the benefits [they realize].

I think this is the biggest return that you can get from what you are doing. To get to the point where you understand or realize what to do and how to create this success—this is really the joy of the creation of this. You get to that point—and you have to have a lot of them along the way—until you get to a company that has a good product with a great customer base, and, pretty much, it's on its way to success. I believe that the founder has something to do with every step of the way, because you have this certain vision that started this whole thing. Everything else that you've done along the way has to be aligned with this vision.

That's another reward you get as a founder, and it's a comfort to know that you have a lot invested in all these tools, these services that your customers are using. We are talking, for example, about helping restaurants have better, healthier businesses. Helping those 700,000 single-owner restaurants in the U.S.—they have probably about twenty to thirty employees. You help them make sure the business is healthy and positive, that they have the money to pay the employees, have the money to hire more, and be more successful with additional places. You have your hands in all of that. That's a huge return.

Guy: At the beginning [of this interview], I said none of my technology companies [failed]; we didn't close them, but I don't know how much of a success they were. But yes, this was a business that actually failed.

Maybe that's why I'm here now—because you're right: Maybe my failure caused me to go out there and say, "Okay, I need to turn this one into an opportunity."

I was super lucky, because I know we sold it for a little bit less than what we invested in it. It was a loss, but it wasn't a big one. We were able to move on to the next thing. Yes, absolutely—these are very important things that I went through.

Lalia: What have you learned from this experience?

Guy: First of all, to only go into businesses where I have complete access to the right data on hand to make the decisions that can pretty much decide whether it will be a success or a failure.

From failure, it's important to know when I should be persistent to continue the business and try to get it to a point where it's becoming a successful one, [compared] to when I'm looking at this and saying, "It's going to be too costly." Then we're going to need more money from my investors, and I don't know if I can turn it into a successful, profitable business and give them the return they're looking for.

Lalia: That's a great story. Did you have any goal-setting strategies that you used in your work?

Guy: Actually, that is something that has changed. To be honest, you brought up something that made me think about it. And it's something to change. When I started, I was in a New York company; I did it for a few years, and I had very realistic goals. I was able to achieve them, and then I started raising money in Silicon Valley. I got very unrealistic expectations from people, from dreamers, from other entrepreneurs. The first thing is I really didn't understand how these people were making money, because they're really [just] dreaming; they're not from the same planet I was. I was right—I was from the New York planet, and they were from the Silicon Valley planet.

But, very quickly, you look at that, and you ask: "You know, where are the most successful start-up companies coming from? Silicon Valley." And that's probably because these people have big dreams.

So, let's *not* be afraid for a second. Let's see what can happen if we start dreaming and stop being so realistic. Let's have dreams—let's have unrealistic goals and see how we can solve this challenge. That was only in the beginning—2015—and then we did it. The change that we went through in the last year, especially in the last four months, was triggered by that change in thinking. I actually started to think about it like: "Instead of a thousand customers, I want to hit ten thousand customers." It didn't sound realistic to me. If somebody else [had heard] me, they would say, "Oh, this guy is a dreamer. He's dangerous—he doesn't have his feet on the ground." But when we actually started challenging that and saying,

"Let's see how we can be realistic with these dreams," we were able to overachieve even the goals that we set.

Lalia: Did you do any planning where you would ask, "What are the steps we have to take?"

Guy: Yes. I think one of the things that changes is [that you start asking]—"What are the steps? What can I do now, moving forward, and where is it going to get me?" When you consider what you have already or what you've learned so far, then, yes—you're going to get to something very predictive. But then you say, "What do I need to get to ten thousand customers within the next twelve months?" As unrealistic as it is, I really need to do that. So how can I do it?"

Now you start asking, "Is this going to get me there? No. Is this going to get me there? No. What I have is not good enough." Then I have to come up with new ways of doing this. It's actually for us to prove that it works. We experienced very high growth in a very short time, and now, we move into the next step, which is, "How do we monetize on that? This is what we did before, but let's think about other ways. Maybe there are other ways to do that so that we benefit everybody around us." I think—so this is actually what you just mentioned—*This has been a process in the last eighteen months that has radically changed for me.*

As I said before, we actually reached our goals by considering what we know and what we know how to do, by setting up goals and seeing how we can achieve them. I think you know the second way is probably a Silicon Valley way. That's why you have these great companies achieving amazing things in a very short time.

Lalia: Do you ever think about obstacles that might get in your way or what might go wrong?

Guy: You always have to have other options. It's like a chess game when you're making a move. You're making the move, but now you have maybe five other options, and then it's going to multiply—and then it's exponential. Then, you're going to have your opponent make his move. Now you actually have probably twenty-five other options from the previous moves. So yes, you always have to do that. You always have to make sure that you have other options. And [think], "What's going to happen if…" and be prepared. The challenges may be different from what you expected, but it doesn't matter, because you've already thought about it—you've thought about a lot of them, and you're prepared for that.

Lalia: What do you think is the single most important personal factor that contributes to your success as an entrepreneur?

Guy: The top one is passion. Passion to solve the problem; passion to make things better. That's what really drives all of this. It's super challenging along the way. You have ups and downs. You don't give up. You're able to stick it out *only if the passion is there*. It's going to motivate you to go through these challenges; you'll probably have a clearer picture of what's next—you'll know how much better it's going to be in the future.

■ ■ ■ ■ ■

Key Strategies: Guy Praisler

CHANGE YOUR PERSPECTIVE

One of my favorite aspects of Guy's philosophy is his ability to rename things, thereby turning them from a negative to a positive.

It's a rare and wonderful sort of alchemy. By tweaking his terminology, he can alter his view of the many pain-points that arise when starting a business. For instance, Guy refers to failures as "success learnings." In so doing, he erases the many negative connotations of "failure" and lends an actionable, positive tone to any challenging developments. In turn, what first seemed a stop sign now becomes a map to the road ahead.

EXCHANGE YOUR DOUBTS FOR OPPORTUNITIES

Guy views the doubts and fears that accompany any new business as promising little blessings, signposts of potential success. They are opportunities in disguise, signaling the way toward innovation. For instance, Guy's failed restaurant venture yielded the inspiration for Dine Market. If he had succumbed to frustration, allowed that one defeat to hinder his tenacity, he might never have reached his current success. Guy sees the lack of failure as a bad sign. Why? Because it means you aren't even *trying*. So, when you're experiencing doubt or worry, ask yourself, "What innovative opportunity lies hidden behind this fear?"

IDENTIFY YOUR SUPPORT SYSTEM

Guy identifies the three crucial circles/tiers of support vital to an entrepreneur's success: immediate family, friends and extended family, and investors/consultants. His immediate family's support allows him to enjoy a healthy and appropriate work/family life balance. From the second support tier, friends and other family members, he gains additional support and occasional professional advice. Finally, investors and consultants provide him with invaluable advice and mentorship necessary to engage in successful decision-making.

FIND YOUR EUPHORIA

Before tackling a tricky problem, Guy likes to go for a run. He knows from practice and experience that getting in touch with his euphoria will lend a more positive cast to the challenge he is trying to resolve. It's a proven strategy, too: Research has verified that a positive state of mind yields better decision-making and problem-solving. So, ask yourself, what is the source of *your* euphoria? And how can you best access it?

OPTIMISM

Optimism, like persistence, will be a common theme among the entrepreneurs in this book, but some have different definitions. When you read what Guy has to say about being an optimist, you'll see how that one quality overlaps with all the others he notes as essential.

Optimism is the thing that gets the business off the ground in the first place: It's the elementary belief that your idea *can* work and that it *will* work. Guy believes that there is always a choice; there's always something you can do. This belief plays a fundamental role in his persistence and stubbornness. By believing there is always a solution, you'll find one. Sometimes, that solution might be to change directions, but that's still a solution.

His idea of questioning small successes and failures can make it easier to be optimistic about your business, because it leads you to solve problems before they cost you something. To Guy, being an optimist doesn't mean turning a blind eye to obstacles. It means looking for those obstacles and always believing that they can be overcome, removed, or worked through.

MINDSET EXERCISES

GET PHYSICAL

When you need a physical and emotional "pick me up."

- What are the benefits to you when you're more physically active?
- How can you identify what kind of physical activity works best for you?
- What are the criteria that doing this particular physical activity has to meet—e.g., time, location?
- Does it help you to engage in this activity with others?
- How will your productivity increase if you are physically active?
- How much do you really need to be physically active for your well-being?
- What kind of routine will help you incorporate physical activity into your schedule?

SUCCESS LEARNINGS

When you need to regain confidence after a failure.

- What have been some of your professional or personal failures?

- What can you learn from these failures?
- How can you think of these failures as successes?
- How can you take advantage of these "learnings" to help you succeed now?
- How have these failures made you a better entrepreneur?

BUILD YOUR SUPPORT SYSTEM

When you feel like you are an "island."

- Describe all the people you consider to be part of your support system.
- How do they help you succeed in achieving your goals?
- Create three circles:
    - Inner circle—immediate family
    - Second circle—larger family, close friends, and peers
    - Third circle—investors, advisors, consultants
- From which circle do you need to gain more support?
- How would having more support help you succeed?
- How can you build stronger relationships and communication at each level so that they can support you even more?

Think Not About the Problem, but About the Solution

GREG KIMMA

CTO and CFO of InstaMaids

InstaMaids—an online home-cleaning and maid service

Lalia: How did you start InstaMaids?

Greg: After I started at school, that's when I heard about all the start-ups and how well they were doing. I hadn't done anything about it until my friend Darren came up with this idea. My dream, really, is to start my own company, create an app.

Lalia: Do you have a sense of purpose to do something for the world?

Greg: I want to create a nonprofit for kids. Create an environment that is a safe place for kids and [where they can] get some life skills. That's why I want to build a company. A lot of the founders, like

Bill Gates, genuinely want to help the world. Some people want just to make a lot of money.

Lalia: Did you find many obstacles and challenges when you started a business with your best friend?

Greg: A lot of people ask that. There were a few times when we were butting heads and cursing each other out and yelling. Some of the challenges are relational issues. There are many ways to get to an end goal. Because of that, two people might have different ideas. While you are doing that, you don't realize that you are going down the same path. We were doing so many different things. What I learned was that both of us hold things in; we are tough guys who don't express our feelings.

Lalia: What do you view as the challenges to starting a business?

Greg: The business was started about three years ago. You have to treat it like a game. There are a lot of people in boot camp who can't handle that. *(Gregory was a sergeant in the United States Marine Corps.)* I would tell them that it is just a game.

Lalia: In your business, do you ever have doubts?

Greg: In the beginning, I never wanted to do a house-cleaning business. [I am fortunate to have] started with my friend. He has the drive, and he kept me going. You have these clients who are awful. In spite of doing everything for them, they go on Yelp and give you bad reviews. There *will be* times like that—it's tough.

Lalia: What pulls you out of those moments of doubt?

Greg: Just thinking that it would leave Darren high and dry. Because he is working so hard, it would hurt him.

Lalia: What are your coping strategies?

Greg: I think, at first, I was bottling things up. It wasn't good; but, now, I've learned to be better with expressing my feelings. Bottling things up, exploding, and yelling at each other wasn't a good coping strategy. Right now, if there is a stressor, we talk about it. It's great for us that we have a support system. My business partner is my support system. We are both working toward the same thing.

Lalia: What are your personal strengths that are useful for your business?

Greg: I'm an introvert but a people person. In general, people get along with me, and I get along with people. First of all, I don't judge them, and that helps them in trusting me. They can feel in my body language that I am not judging them. They can relax with me; they don't have to put up a persona, and they can just be themselves. Because of that, I feel I make a connection. So, the maids that we have, they might have a hard time adjusting if we change the software or change the way we pay them—all that stuff is constantly changing. So, I meet with them in person and talk with them to make sure everything is okay.

Lalia: What are some of your other strengths that are useful?

Greg: I am good at problem-solving. Things are constantly changing in a business. When you start, and you have a path—and I think it is a good idea to have a path—if you try to stick to this path, you get constantly stressed out, thinking about how you are going to stay on the path. But if you keep your mind constantly adaptable to that path, you'll understand that things are constantly changing. If you get stuck, if you are inflexible, you are going to break. You try out a lot of things with the business. We tried putting a lot of money into it, and it didn't work out, and you have to bend.

Lalia: How do you deal with failure?

Greg: What's good about failure is that you know that, when you fail, you are going to learn something from it. Failure is teaching you something. I look at failure as not necessarily a good thing but as a necessary evil.

Years back, I read quotations about never giving up. It's really true that the people who are successful never give up. They keep their heads down and focused on the path.

Lalia: You said you are an optimist. I love the way you described an optimist.

Greg: I am always thinking about what can go right. My dad always thinks about what can go wrong. Sometimes dad thinks I am not a realist. Sometimes he thinks that I am not addressing the things that can go wrong. He is just concerned that I can get hurt. It's tough to hear these things, *and* it's tough to push through it. In the world, in general, that's what you hear. People always talk about being alert to things, that it is impossible to start your own business, that you are going to lose a lot of money.

Lalia: There is an innate negativity bias. There is also biological optimism. People still go ahead. Tell me about a positive thing that happened in your business.

Greg: Revenues had plateaued. That's when the stress started to happen. We were trying different things, and it was tough. Finally, in the last four months, the revenue went up. I was able to keep at it, and, eventually, it started working when we streamlined.

Lalia: What caused the bad events? What did you feel was beyond your control?

Greg: Trying to please everyone is beyond our control. The customers don't like the maids, or the maids get offended if they have been asked to do something.

Lalia: What did you learn from your difficulties?

Greg: Talking about what went wrong and what went right with my business partner really helped. We can brainstorm around the problems that repeat. A lot of our problems have diminished. Now we are thinking about the future. Before, we were putting out fires.

Lalia: Do you have any goal-setting strategies?

Greg: Our goal was not to go bankrupt. We were spending all our time on that. We hired customer service. Now we can focus on moving forward. Now, we are free to build what we can in order to grow.

Lalia: Do you look at obstacles and brainstorm on how to get around them?

Greg: We have done a lot of focusing on what can go wrong, but maybe not enough. We didn't have enough in place—that is why Los Angeles fell apart.

Lalia: Are you determined?

Greg: Definitely—I want to make a path.

Lalia: What's your strategy when something gets in your way?

Greg: I try not to let it bother me. I feel I am really good at problem-solving, troubleshooting. I think not about the problem, but about the solution.

Lalia: Does that help you?

Greg: I have the confidence to know I have a solution. I see it as a puzzle to solve. For some, it's a wall; for others, it's like picking locks. I don't take things personally. If you take things personally, you are dead in the water. Pessimists ruminate, so [the problem] snowballs. I am able to disconnect from other people's problems.

■ ■ ■ ■ ■

Key Strategies: Greg Kimma

YOUR PARTNER IS YOUR BEST SUPPORT

Greg partnered with a friend to launch InstaMaids. When things turned rocky, that partnership helped solidify his commitment to the business. Their mutual support provides both accountability and creative problem-solving. Greg knows that such relationships take considerable effort by managing their differences through candid communication, mutual trust, and open collaboration.

LEVERAGE YOUR STRENGTHS TO BUILD YOUR BUSINESS

Greg holds an accurate and clear-eyed understanding of his personal strengths. Reflecting on his strengths, he describes himself as a "people person." This quality benefits his management style, where he builds strong one-on-one relationships with his workers. His support and non-judgment help them manage customers' expectations and complaints. As such, he serves the overall good of the business by ensuring vital customer service.

His training as a Marine has helped him foster the necessary grit and resilience required of an entrepreneur. For reinforcement of these strengths, he nourishes himself with inspirational quotations that fortify this persistence and determination.

THINK OF IT AS A GAME

This one sounds counterintuitive, almost cavalier. Not so for Greg. He utilized this mental strategy to succeed at the Marine boot camp's uniquely grueling process, and he has successfully guided others into adopting the same mindset. By reframing challenges in such a fashion, you can draw on your natural sense of competitiveness and playfulness to get through them successfully.

When embracing the spirit of game-play, you remind yourself that, sure, you're in it to win, but you may also lose, and that's okay. It's strategic and creative but also playful.

HOLD FAST TO OPTIMISM

Greg likes to practice optimism by focusing his thinking on the things that can go right. It doesn't mean that he entirely disregards obstacles or challenges. Together with his partner, they try to foresee all eventualities and prepare to confront them. When Greg encounters a challenge, he thinks about possible solutions rather than the problem itself. When viewed with optimism, problems are puzzles to be solved or locks to be picked. They are momentary, not permanent, challenges.

MINDSET EXERCISES

GET INSPIRED

When you need a quick burst of inspiration, motivation, and self-confidence.

- Who are some of your favorite professional and personal heroes?
- What is it about them that inspires you?
- What are some of your favorite famous quotes that give you a boost?
- Is there a theme that regularly occurs in these favorites?
- What can you do to get quick access to these quotes when things get tough?
- How can you apply them to your work and life?

GET A GOOD THINKING PARTNER/ SOUNDING BOARD

When you need feedback and counterpoints to make better decisions.

- Do you often find yourself feeling like you are out there alone when making tough decisions?

- Do you have a partner, advisor, or mentor who can be your sounding board and with whom you can exchange ideas, dispute issues, analyze problems, brainstorm creative ideas, and engage in critical thinking?

- If you don't have that person, how can you find one?

- Who can you rely on to get some critical feedback?

- How can you be more open to asking for and getting feedback?

- What communication skills do you need to improve upon to engage with that person even better?

GET SOLUTION-FOCUSED, AND MOVE THE DIAL

When you are stuck in a problem and need to be solution-focused.

- Think of a problem that you are facing currently. What is the outcome that you would like to see?

- On a scale of 1-10 (with 1 representing the worst it can be and 10 being the best), where are you right now on the path toward solving that problem and achieving that outcome?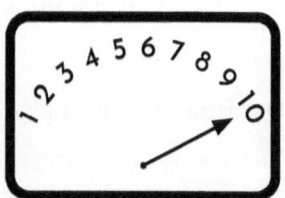

- Assuming your rating was more than 1, ask yourself what factors contributed to it not being the worst-case scenario. How did you contribute to that?

- Start with thinking about moving one notch up on the scale toward the outcome.

- Is there anything you can build on to increase the rating?
- Describe what would be better if the rating were higher.
- Now, what is the next thing you need to do to move toward solving the problem right now?
- Where on the scale are you now in terms of how you are viewing the problem?

The Goal Is to Win the Game

IDDO TAL

CEO, Co-founder of Invi Labs, Inc.

Invi Messaging—a smart messaging app that allows users to share media as interactive content within text messages

Lalia: I was at Founders World, and I heard you speak. I loved your enthusiasm and your positive spirit. I thought it would be great to get a little bit into your head about the way you deal with challenges and the way you deal with overcoming your obstacles.

Briefly, give me a little overview of your different start-ups, the successes, and the failures.

Iddo: The one before Invi.com was a high-frequency financial trading application company, which was a very profitable company. It's the first time something generated a lot of worth and revenues and allowed me to accumulate wealth—but certainly not to the extent that I don't need to work anymore. Almost like you are hungry, and, now, finally, you have a good meal in a good restaurant. You know how it feels, you know how it tastes, and, now, you want more. That's how I felt after that venture.

Before that, I created a social network for events. Before that, I created TV.TV, which is a peer-to-peer metric for distributing TV. And, before that, I created Send to Post, which is [like an extension of the concept of the "Send" button in email]. We added "Send to Post," the first cloud solution for printing.

I have invested in some start-ups, and I've helped some others. Every morning I wake up, I have two more ideas.

Lalia: That's a common thing I hear from a lot of entrepreneurs.

Iddo: A few months ago, we went to Zion Park. We went through Vegas, and my wife said, "Let's stay in Vegas. We'll see a show." After the morning with the kids at the swimming pool, I took the rest of the day to find an accelerator, a shared working space for start-ups in Vegas, met start-ups and investors, and spent the whole day there. That's my passion.

Lalia: Of all those things that you have done, you must have experienced both failures and successes.

Iddo: Yes, definitely. Churchill said that the definition of success is moving from failure to failure without losing your excitement. This is looking at the big scheme of things. But if you look at every second in the day, every hour in the day, it's "measure-learn-repeat." We have a big poster near the developers that says just that. There is no failure—there is only learning experiences. For me, going on stage the other day was a learning experience. Remember the guy before me?

Lalia: I don't remember who was before you.

Iddo: I think another 600 people will not remember him. He was whispering. The people in the audience were all attached to their phones, and no one remembered him. This was what I had to follow. What I'm saying is, it was a challenge. If I had continued after him in a regular voice, no one would have listened. I had to be a bit of a trouble-maker, to attract all the attention and then deliver my message. Then I'm the lucky guy—the one you remember—and not him. This is what I mean by "experience." This is learning. It is about having the experience and then anticipating what's going to happen next.

Lalia: What are the keys in terms of your mindset to help you get through difficult times?

Iddo: One is positive thinking. The second is a supportive environment—in my case, my wife. If you look at the research about people who live past the age of ninety-five, there were two dominant things present: optimistic, positive thinking and eating small quantities of food. Since I eat a lot of food, I need to be really positive. The second, as they say in French, *"Cherchez la femme"*—"look for the woman." You can't do it without your partner, and your partner needs to understand that. When a partner marries an entrepreneur, he or she is totally immersed in what you're doing. There are ups, and there are downs. You cannot do it without a supporting partner. When you have your biggest nightmare, you need the partner to say, "I believe in you. Make it happen. You made it last time, and you're going to make it this time." When you don't believe in yourself, [you must have] someone who does.

Lalia: Did you ever feel like giving up?

Iddo: Many times. I think that a good night's sleep and some support is what I need in order to wake up and get going again.

Lalia: What have been your major stress points in terms of your start-ups?

Iddo: I think the biggest one is thinking that you are going nowhere, that the product is no good, and that there is competition. With that mindset, you're not going to make it. Then, you also have the commitment that you made to investors, to yourself, to people around you, to your target audience, and to your customers. They are thinking that you're not good enough and that you are probably not going to make it.

Lalia: How do you manage those kinds of thoughts and feelings?

Iddo: You put yourself back in a beautiful state. For me, I go to sleep, wake up early in the morning, exercise a lot, and get into peak state. It's almost like getting to the zone, focused. Also, understanding the outcome and the purpose. Once I remember the purpose—why I'm here, why I'm doing this—I get the emotional juice to run forward.

Lalia: Can you give me some specifics when you talk about understanding your purpose?

Iddo: My purpose in life is to touch and improve the lives of millions of people and to empower dramatically. I want to make a living, and I want to take my kids to Disneyland, but that's not the purpose of my life. My purpose in life is to create amazing things. It starts from the core. It's me, then my wife, then my kids, and then my surroundings—and it becomes a snowball of how I touch people.

What guides me has always been, *How can I make things better?* There is a constant drive inside me to improve things. It's minimal footprint and maximum impact. How can I do as little as I can that will make a huge impact? That's constantly in my mind.

Lalia: When you're faced with difficulties—maybe it's not failures, but obstacles—in your work, do you find yourself getting back to that sense of purpose in order to help you through that?

Iddo: It's where your focus is and your language that really impacts your state of mind. I put myself in a good mood and make myself happy. Then I remind myself of my purpose. Usually, that brings me into a beautiful state, a peak state, where I'm happy. It's almost like, if you're in a bad mood, you buy a nice shirt. It helps you get into a good mood. Those external things affect your mood. I also identify bad or constant patterns and triggers of fears, negative thoughts, or judgments of others or myself. I identify the pattern; I stop it, and then I replace it with a good thought. It's almost like rewiring myself.

Lalia: There's a lot to worry about, isn't there, when you're creating a start-up?

Iddo: Once I'm totally immersed in something, I'm in a beautiful state, and I usually achieve my goals. When I have the purpose in mind, it's beautiful. At one point, there is almost like a happy, divine intervention. You can call it God, angels, my grandma. Everyone can call it a different thing, but there is some sort of a divine something that is amazing that happens when you don't expect it. Some people call it *luck*. Some people say luck is when preparation meets opportunity.

With the start-up that I had, I said, "I'm going to do it. I don't care. I'm going to do the right thing." Then good things [started happening] without me even realizing it. The other day, I went to the bank [to get cash]. I said to myself, "Why don't they give me some more?" It was a joke in my head. I came home, and, literally, the woman who had cashed the money had given me a thousand dollars more.

I was shocked. I counted it again. I went to the online bank account, and it showed a withdrawal of $9,000, but I had $10,000. The next morning, I stopped at the bank, and I asked the manager, "Joe, are you missing a thousand dollars?" He said, "Oh, my gosh! We worked late. We all counted because we were missing a thousand dollars." "She gave me an extra thousand dollars by mistake," I told him.

On the way back, I was working out how I would raise money for my start-up. It was [still in the] early stages, and I started singing to myself this word in Hebrew that means "eighty times." When you do something good, you get eighty times for it. I was happy. I was in a good mood; I did something good. I got home, and I got on my computer; I had two emails. One was from Ariel Spivak, who is [a] high-level [player] in Google biz development. He said, "Iddo, I want to put $20,000 into the company." Then there was another email from Shaq. After that, Ashton Kutcher invested in the start-up, and then, after that, all his friends. The $80,000 I got just for the thousand I gave back. Eighty times more. These stories happen, and you can call it the *instant karma of Silicon Valley*. When you do things right, when you have the courage to do the right thing, it pays off.

Lalia: I love that story. Where do you think your personal strengths come from that are useful for being an entrepreneur?

Iddo: Wow—I want to say it's genetic or education. My father was always there for me. Some of my friends have more educated parents, richer, smarter, more handsome. One thing my father had is that, first, he was a good model of positive relationships at home—[he had] a true, real, passionate friendship with my mom. Second, he was always there for me when I needed him. Even now, when I'm an adult, he is always there. I need him less and less, but when I need him, he is always there, always listening. When you have a supportive environment, you know that whatever happens, it's almost as if you have a safety net.

Lalia: What do you think your personal strengths are, especially in terms of being an entrepreneur and going through all the ups and downs?

Iddo: I don't give up. I'm a fighter. I don't give up. I also wake up in the morning optimistic and get right into it. I'm very playful. I fool around and do this, and I don't let it touch me.

Lalia: You have these great strengths. What are your weaknesses, if you don't mind revealing them?

Iddo: I think that one of the things I really need to work on is my English. It is my second language. I see the young kids here in Palo Alto— even my son, who is in fourth grade—and how rich their language and vocabulary are and how amazingly they do in writing. I also don't have a technical background in a product business. If I had a technical background, I would be much stronger. There are so many things like those. They don't hold me back, but it would be a higher place to jump from.

Lalia: Do you find that you use your strengths to overcome your weaknesses?

Iddo: Yes, for sure. The creative thinking and learning to create crucial conversations with people—they [make up for] all the characteristics that I don't have. Also, in a start-up, once you're an entrepreneur, it's almost like you do everything by yourself. I know I'm not a designer, and [I know] I'm not a good programmer. Eventually, you start getting very strong people, and I believe in transformational leadership. I believe in leading them, not managing them. You bring really strong people, you make them co-founders, and you create the right game for them to thrive. Then the team compensates for your weaknesses.

Lalia: That's critical. You describe yourself as an optimist. Tell me a little bit more about what that means to you.

Iddo: It's almost as if—if you put in enough focus and there is a purpose, you can really visualize the outcome; it can be done. You think about it, you talk about it, and you say, "There is going to be a house there. It is going to have two floors. There is going to be these windows, and this is the plan." Eventually, there is going to be a house there. You convince everyone around you that there is going to be a house there, but there isn't—*yet*. Through believing, pushing, not stopping, and dealing with all the obstacles, eventually, there is a house there. Understand that the words are there before the reality—and that's okay. That's the right order.

It's all a game. It's all a story in our heads. If it's all really a story and we just put the meaning into it, why wouldn't we put a beautiful meaning on it and just create something amazing? [You come to] understand that it's all a game, that it's just stories in your head.

Lalia: As an optimist, how do you view negative events that happened in any of your start-ups?

Iddo: In 2008, the [entire] market collapsed. [But, then, again,] it had already collapsed in 2001, when I created my first start-up. That was the dotcom bust. [During that one] I was in a VC office for a month already. They did due diligence with the term sheet, and then they came back. They sent a junior employee to say, "Iddo, we're taking back the term sheet. We will not invest." I'm the optimistic guy, and I acted really fast. I was depressed, and I went to sleep. I woke up early in the morning, and I rushed like crazy to raise money. I grabbed $5 million from Omnicom Group, the largest advertising agency.

We were the last ones to take the money. After that, everything collapsed, and I stopped my MBA right in the middle. All the guys who finished MBAs four months later couldn't find a job for five years, and I was a CEO of forty employees, with half a million in the bank. Isn't it crazy? That's [an example of] when you "experience and anticipate."

The next time, when the market was about to go down, I sensed it. We had founded a high-frequency financial trading company, and when the market collapsed, we made a lot of money. There was no liquidity, and we put liquidity into the market. Even when something bad happens, if you anticipate it, you can cash in on it. That's, I think, the wisdom of experience. You just learn. The first time, I was lucky, I was rushing with intuition, but the second time, I was really getting ready for it. Sometimes you can anticipate; sometimes, you're surprised, and sometimes, there is [what seems like] divine [intervention].

For everything that happens to you that you cannot control, there is something else you can control, and that affects the outcome of that thing.

Lalia: How do you set goals? What do you think about them? You talked a lot about outcomes and having a vision of something.

Iddo: I imagine the outcome. I visualize it and talk about it obsessively to others. I call them "my victims." "Mom, how are you? I have a new idea." I talk with her about it, and I totally visualize in the conversation. My mom loves to listen, but when she cannot listen anymore, I say, "Thank you, Mom. Now, I will go to another victim." After three, four, five, ten people, I relax. I've verbalized it so many times that it's almost like an incantation, and I'm [very] clear in every conversation. The person will ask one or two questions that totally take me to the next level and the next level. Now, I see it so detailed, so vivid, so alive, and I have a plan.

Lalia: Do you find yourself setting goals and attaching a certain date to their completion? Do you find yourself planning the steps?

Iddo: I like to call them "outcomes." I don't like to call them "goals." *Outcomes*—there is *always* an outcome. The goals can change. I'll do something, and it can be a miserable outcome if nothing happens. It could be a beautiful outcome—it could be an outstanding outcome—but there *is* going to be an outcome. *Goals*—I don't know. They're not so connected. It's just a goal. A goal is almost like talking about the price. "I need to do this, and I need to do that. This is the thing I need." What's empowering me is what I'm going to achieve.

Lalia: You have to have steps. You have to have goals for the people working for you.

Iddo: *Outcomes* that they are going to reach; then we visualize it, and then we celebrate it.

Lalia: There is the thing called SMART goals. Have you heard of SMART goals? It's an acronym for Specific, Measurable, Attainable, Relevant, and then "T" is *timely*—within the right time frame.

Iddo: Yeah. That's a strategy. I'll tell you what I'm more connected with. November of last year was a very stressful time for me. The company and things were not going well, and I needed to create a big, massive shift on a personal level. I was told, "You're almost pre-diabetic. Your cholesterol is high. The fat level in your blood is high. You need to take care of yourself." I got very stressed. I was jogging every day, and I still had that happen. I was already jogging forty-five minutes a day almost every day.

I could have gone for measurable goals. All these scary things are very hard for me to follow through on. But, still, I can relax, accept myself, and say, "Something happened. First, let's relax. Let's enjoy. Let's breathe. Let's see what the purpose here is." My purpose here is to feel vivid, alive, energetic. If my temple, my body, is not functioning well, I can't do anything else. This needs to be the first priority.

Five months later, I was living a healthy lifestyle. I shed I think eighteen or twenty pounds. I went to my physician for a blood test, and she was shocked. She said, "What did you do? I want to do the same." I was totally normal. I think my biggest achievement was [bringing] those numbers down. [I had to] create a lifestyle that sustains it. I could stress myself with splitting timelines and measurements and all of this. I could be too serious with myself and not be kind with myself. It doesn't mean that I am not taking massive action. Those methods we are talking about are not right for me. It is almost like making the method [more] important [than] the outcome. You want to get to the hill. If you go down and you find out that there is a different route that is much easier, that's [not necessarily] ideal. You don't want to make the method holy.

Lalia: When you've got some kind of an outcome in one of your businesses, you're working toward it somehow—and not only in small, measurable, achievable goals on your way.

Iddo: You measure all the time. It's not that you are not measuring, but you *can be* playful with it.

Lalia: That's true, because you said that you have that playfulness in how you do things.

Iddo: Yes. Be *authentic* with yourself. Set for yourself the outcome that you want to achieve—and just go do it. Give yourself a bit of slack [in deciding what the best way to do it is]. Don't be harsh with yourself if you don't achieve a small milestone on the way. See the big picture. That's what you want to have, because sometimes it takes you eighty percent of the time to do the first ten percent, and then you sit down one evening and do the rest.

It's important for me to know that, when I lead people, I give them slack as well. We have something called Jira [software development tool]. We work in sprints. We have points. We have gamification for the work process. It's very organized. I took it to a JIRA master, and I wrote an amazing blog about it. Then I found that I don't totally believe in what I wrote. It was a big thing. If I showed you the blog, you would say, "You totally nailed how Agile development methodology should work—setting goals and measurement." Some people are so focused on the process that they miss the boat. There is an art—Yin and Yang, the balance between the two. Art and science.

Lalia: It turns out that there are a lot of people who have created start-ups and get very disheartened, get depressed, even commit suicide, actually. What would you say to somebody who's having a hard time? You've helped other entrepreneurs. You've probably run into people who aren't as upbeat and optimistic as you by nature.

Iddo: I think that every person has an entrepreneurial part of their personality. Everyone has a place to express themselves. You see an entrepreneur, and you know that they want to make it big time. They are totally focused. They are in the right space. They are doing it for the right purpose. They are trying to build themselves correctly to get to a point.

Some people who are depressed have made the wrong choices. Some of them are driven for the wrong reasons. Some of them are trying to do things that are very hard for them—they are doing them for irrelevant reasons, instead of what is easy for them. I had a guy who left his job. He was already consulting for a start-up. He wanted to get into it, and I saw that it was an area he understood nothing about. He was going to fail. He didn't have the background. It was clear that he was going to have huge obstacles. Instead of that, he threw in a third idea, and he's passionate about that one. I said, "This is better suited to you." After twenty minutes of conversation, he made his decision to let go completely and to focus on one thing.

He even went online, and we found a domain for it. He purchased the name. That was four months ago, and, yesterday, he came here, and he is already advanced. He is radiant and passionate and full of energy, because he went to something that he feels is totally in his control, his area of expertise. It's easy for him. He can bring explosive value there very easily.

If somebody is really suffering, then, probably, they are in the wrong space. It happens a lot. Even to me, sometimes. It's okay to understand that there are things that you cannot do. It's very tempting for an entrepreneur to just jump in, hands-on, and try to do everything.

Lalia: What would your advice be for someone who's become disheartened or depressed?

Iddo: First of all, move, jump, dance. Do something physical. Do something good for you. If it's ice cream, it needs to be healthy—from fruits. Put some greens into it, with a smile.

Then change your terminology. Change the meaning of the story that you're telling yourself. Shake off the pattern-thinking that says something can't be done and that you will not make it. You need to change to something optimistic. Change the words and your focus, and really be honest with yourself in choosing to do something that's easy for you. Think: "This is so easy, I can't believe they're paying me for this. I'd do this for free." That's the way you want to be.

Lalia: There is one last question that came to me as you were talking about this. You're optimistic, but there is this thing called *realistic optimism*. Do you see value in really checking and focusing, making sure that you're not being foolish?

Iddo: Yes, and I have few tips for that. One is measure. Whatever you do, measure. See the outcome. Second, have a peer group or have a mentor. Find somebody who did what you want to do and succeeded in it, and just attach yourself to that person. The way to attach yourself to that person is to give them an explosive value. Find what they need, and just give it to them like there is no tomorrow. Learn. Have a peer group who's going through the same thing with whom you can consult, and maybe a coach who will kick your butt when you get too comfortable.

Remember that it's a game and that our goal is to win the game. You want to play. Be playful. Try from here, try from there, and then go back and try again—and marry well.

■ ■ ■ ■ ■

Key Strategies: Iddo Tal

GET INTO THE RIGHT STATE

When Iddo starts to feel overloaded, he likes to change his state. He allows himself a physical reset—a "rewiring of the brain," he calls it. It's a simple tip and an actionable one. By altering and improving his physiology, he cultivates a better frame of mind. The first step: a good night's sleep. Next, upon rising, he exercises, clearing his head and creating mental space for the difficult tasks before him that day. It's a proven strategy, too: There exists an abundant and growing body of research to support the importance of the body/mind connection. In short, healthier physicality aids in resilience, focus, and determination.

According to Iddo, any entrepreneur feeling the creep of distress should carve out time for whatever activity might trigger that mental reboot. You can go for a jog or a hike, dance, play music, or engage in any activity that generates an upbeat mood and starts the positivity flowing again. Even indulging in a bit of healthy ice cream (with fruit) can help.

Similarly, devising and articulating a vision of your desired goal can prove beneficial, too. Visualize it, and verbalize it. Iddo uses the example of building a house. Even the simple act of describing the structure elicits a physiological response—"that feeling in your body." Sometimes such a reset process is all that's required to find your joy again.

MAINTAIN YOUR PURPOSE, PASSION, AND VALUES

By connecting with his purpose, Iddo can guide himself into a positive state, allowing him to access what he's dubbed "the divine zone"—a mindset of joy and contentment.

For Iddo, a relentless focus on his values—improving the lives of others and doing the "right thing"—opens doors for him by seeming magic. By way of example, he related an anecdote about returning money to the bank, after which investments came flowing in, like water from a mystical geyser. It's "Silicon Valley luck," he says.

In a more practical sense, by prioritizing his values, Iddo can make effective choices on where to allocate his precious time and energy. Whether he's bonding with family, mentoring entrepreneurs or guiding his employees, Iddo constantly consults his inner compass, that intrinsic sense of what's important and best serves his values. As Iddo tells it, articulating the purpose behind his business has helped attract funding from amazing people all around the globe. His dream, it seems, is wonderfully infectious.

PRIORITIZE OUTCOMES OVER GOALS

Iddo prefers to pursue "outcomes" over "goals." Goals, to his thinking, are more rigidly fixed, whereas an outcome allows room for flexibility and the possibility of adaptation. Guided by purpose, he can mold and re-fashion any given outcome—good, bad, or ugly—into something wholly better.

BE PLAYFUL, BE FLEXIBLE

As with Gregory Kimma, Iddo's personal philosophy reframes the solving of problems as a sort of game to be played. For him, it's a blend of art *and* science—with a dash of fun. Though he has garnered plenty of experience developing systems, including many that were regarded as models of Agile processes, Iddo favors a more artful approach that allows him to explore, iterate, and experiment. The scientific part comes later, with the measurement of results.

MINDSET EXERCISES

FIRE UP YOUR PURPOSE AND PASSION

When you need to fire up your motivation and get going.

- When do you most feel alive and fulfilled?
- What do you love to do that is challenging, energizing, and allows you to lose track of time?
- What matters most to you in your work and life?
- What do you *really, really* want for yourself?
- What do you *really* want for others?
- How would you like to make a difference?
- What are you willing to work your butt off for?
- Why are you doing what you are doing right now?
- What gives you meaning?
- What are some world problems you would like to see solved?
- What would you want to be recognized for?
- What would you be excited about doing tomorrow morning?

FIND YOUR JOY/TAKE A PLAY BREAK

When you are feeling stale, uncreative or you just need a break.

- What's the most fun you have had this past week, month, year?

- What can you do today, this coming week, this month, this year, to take a break from your work and worries?

- In the past, what have you done to spark your creativity?

- When you are in a rut, can you give yourself permission to get away from things and forget about them for a while?

- What can you do to laugh more?

- What can you do to make more play in your life happen?

- When have you last experienced being in a positive state of mind?

- What can you do to experience that state again?

- How will "playing" more impact your work?

- Can you find a "play" buddy with who will help you experience more joy and positivity?

KNOW YOUR VALUES

When you need to find your "why."

- What are the values that you were brought up with?
- Which of them are still important to you?
- Think of times when you had to make choices and decisions. Which values did you use to guide you?
- What values do your heroes have that you identify with?
- Which values that the entrepreneurs in this book mentioned resonated with you?
- Which of their values were meaningful to you?
- From the list on page 102, choose which of these values resonate with you.
- Are there any other values you can think of to add to the list?
- Narrow these down to your top seven.
- Write down what these values mean to you and how you see yourself using them in your work and life.
- Focus on one value for each day of the week, and apply it to everything you do.
- What positive impact did this exercise have on your mindset?

VALUES

Abundance	Decisiveness	Joy	Resilience
Acceptance	Dependability	Kindness	Respect
Accountability	Diversity	Knowledge	Resourcefulness
Achievement	Education	Leadership	Responsibility
Adventure	Empathy	Learning	Responsiveness
Ambition	Encouragement	Love	Risk Taking
Appreciation	Enthusiasm	Loyalty	Safety
Attractiveness	Ethics	Making a Difference	Security
Authenticity	Excellence	Mindfulness	Self-Control
Autonomy	Fairness	Motivation	Selflessness
Balance	Family	Open-Mindedness	Service
Boldness	Fitness	Originality	Simplicity
Brilliance	Flexibility	Passion	Spirituality
Calmness	Freedom	Performance	Stability
Caring	Friendship	Personal Development	Success
Challenge	Generosity	Peace	Thankfulness
Charity	Gratitude	Perfection	Thoughtfulness
Cheerfulness	Growth	Playfulness	Trustworthiness
Cleverness	Happiness	Popularity	Understanding
Collaboration	Health	Positivity	Uniqueness
Community	Honesty	Power	Usefulness
Commitment	Humility	Preparedness	Versatility
Compassion	Humor	Proactivity	Vision
Consistency	Independence	Professionalism	Warmth
Contribution	Individuality	Punctuality	Wealth
Cooperation	Innovation	Quality	Well-Being
Courage	Inspiration	Recognition	Wisdom
Creativity	Intelligence	Relationships	
Curiosity	Intuition	Reliability	

> *Nothing Is Hard –
> Everything Is Doable*

SHAR BEHZADIAN

CEO and Co-founder of TravTribe

TravTribe—supports digital nomads through sharing creative gigs

---

Lalia: Tell me the story about your business and how this all came to be.

Shar: I was born in Iran and moved to Tehran when I was seventeen; I was living alone. That was not normal for a woman to do that alone. I started an import/export company. Then I moved to the U.S. when I was twenty-seven. I did not know anyone here, and I had to figure things out by myself. There were sanctions in Iran, and, so, it was a perfect time to get my graduate degree; so, I [completed my work for] an MBA. San Francisco is a place for innovators, so where would be a better place to go?

I had to create networks of people. I had to find my own resources for things. Believe it or not, it is hard to find out the first things about being here. There are so many international people here, you'd think that there would be many resources available, but there are not. When you are moving to a new country, everything is so exciting that you don't care about how hard it is to find the resources that you need.

Last year, I went to Mexico. I wanted to learn Spanish, and I wanted the experience of jumping into a situation that you don't know anything about and then figuring things out. I wanted to jump into the experience of not knowing a language, and I wanted to learn how to surf. I was nervous. The second I got off the plane, I realized how amazing the people are. I felt local because I met all these people. I experienced a state of happiness that I had not experienced since I was a kid. Waking up to see what would happen, I felt a sense of belonging—even in a community where I did not know anyone. It was an amazing travel experience in my life.

I came back to the U.S. [As I interacted with all the friends that I had made], I realized that they were trapped in this rat race. All of these people here are just chasing after money. But they are not using this money—they are just waiting to go on a vacation once a year.

So, I started talking to people about traveling. Was it just me who experienced that sense of belonging I'd felt in Mexico? I figured that there were many people who want to experience it. So, I thought, *What if I created this for people?* So I started to pursue this idea to create an *authentic* travel experience for people. What if I could create this experience for more people moving to a new country? What if you could quickly become like a local and meet people constantly because those people are immediately available to you when you are moving to a new country? It is just a matter of learning how to communicate with and connect with communities.

Lalia: What do you think made you feel that happiness in Mexico?

Shar: I think happiness is different from the *state of happiness*. In Mexico, I was in this constant state of happiness—carefree, letting things happen to me. Everything was okay. It was like I had the attitude of being ready for anything—fearlessly ready for anything and knowing I would be safe.

I used to have four or five different bracelets on my hand. Each of them stood for a different value for each day. Each one reminded me of something to think about each day. One of them was from my experience in Mexico, and that is to do something every day that scares me. That was a practice for me, a practice to be fearless. Every good thing that happens is a result of that.

Lalia: What makes an entrepreneur have more courage and bounce back from failure? You had your own anchors that helped you do that.

Shar: I had a couple of them. Entrepreneurship is like this—it's a roller coaster. You don't know what to do, and you have to get yourself up and out of this, so every time, you learn how to stand up. After Mexico, I went from a high to a very low. I started having actual pain. I was running around; I wasn't very happy. One night I read Rumi: "God picks up a flute and blows into it, and the music that comes out of it is actually a need that comes out of each of us. Go on the roof and sing your own song and be your own calling." Or something like that. I thought: *Okay, I know my own calling. I am going to start this.* So I created a website that night, and I put my concept on it. I started marketing that concept, and, starting in July, I started to get more subscriptions, feedback, and ideas. This helped me get closer to the concept that I am working on today.

Lalia: Were there ever moments of doubts when you started this? And how did you overcome them?

Shar: My doubt is basically that it's going to take at least three years to get to where I want to be. Is it better to do that? I am in my thirties. Or should I get a job and do the things that are *guaranteed* to get me a result? That is my biggest doubt.

I think the more you learn that you should not care about what society and people expect you to be, the more you depend on what you want to be, and the easier it gets to overcome the doubt. The more you learn to trust yourself, in small ways, the more you learn that trusting yourself actually gives you results. You learn to get over the doubts easily.

Lalia: What are your major stress points? What keeps you up at night?

Shar: Basic problems. Sometimes I get feedback from customers, clients, or my market research, and I freak out. What if what I am doing is not really creating value? What can I improve? The business is customer service, and [success] is very much in the details. So that keeps me up at night. Thinking about solutions, making it happen. Then I solve it, and I sleep.

Lalia: What is one personal trait that you would like to have more of, that would help your business be a success?

Shar: The more successful, the more I am *me*. The more I am living out of myself, really exposing my idea to society, the more successful I get. The more I am me, the more you see passion in my eyes, and I get more results. I want to be completely and utterly out of myself and in the world. Instead of thinking about me, I want to be more on the edge.

Lalia: How do you think about failure?

Shar: Failure to me is not to realize that something does not work and then keep doing it. Success is to realize *quickly* that something does not work and to change it.

Lalia: Do you have any other coping strategies that you use?

Shar: I am very creative. So, I come up with various solutions, and I come up with various problems that need to be solved. Because of that, I am always managing a couple of projects at the same time, in the business and in life in general. The best coping strategies for me are to keep reminding myself of the most important things that need to be done and of the values that help me keep going in my direction.

I remind myself: Always focus on the things you want to create. I have Post-Its in front of my bed. Right now, on the Post-Its are "focus" and "What are the customers' needs?" Before that, it was "Let go." They change from personal life messages to business messages.

Lalia: What are your personal strengths that are useful for being an entrepreneur?

Shar: My personal strengths are that I can jump into an unknown situation and live with chaos—without a manual. I can figure things out, I can define a system, I can identify resources, and I can connect. Basically, in one sentence, my personal strength is to connect, to connect the dots.

Lalia: Do you think of yourself as an optimist?

Shar: I call myself an optimist because I try to see the positive in a situation—but also the negative, so that I change the negative in a way so that I see the positive results. For example, the one question I get asked every day is "What is hard?" That does not mean anything to me. I don't understand the word "hard," because things, jobs, tasks may be time-consuming or slow, but nothing is *hard*—everything is doable. That is how I define optimism.

Lalia: Can you tell me about a positive event that has happened in starting your business?

Shar: A positive event... so many, every day. With our business model, the supply side of the market are the travel users, people who are passionate about traveling off the beaten path. At some point in their lives, they left their ordinary lives and they just went and traveled. I love those people. I want to surround myself with those people. One positive event that I experience every day is that I get to meet those people and hear their stories. That is a high point of my day.

Lalia: What part do you play in making the positive event happen? What do you bring to that?

Shar: Every person has a tribe—they feel happiest when they are in their tribe. My tribe is the traveler tribe, the travelers who spontaneously embrace life and are living every moment. Travel is a very good way of bringing that value of living life to the fullest.

What I did at the very beginning stage was to define their common characteristics, narrow it down, figure out who those people are, and then reach out and find them. The part that I play is listening to their stories, providing them with an opportunity to share their stories with me and with other clients as well, and making that passion contagious.

Lalia: What have been the external factors that have happened in starting your business—like luck, things that you did not have control over?

Shar: For example, I saw my friends here. Stuff like that happens. I see people who I want to meet but don't have access to, and suddenly I meet you, and you have access to them. Or a situation that I imagine actually comes into my life. I have to go there and do my magic—I have to show myself, and I have to work for it.

Lalia: Describe a negative experience that you have had in the process of starting this business.

Shar: I have a hard time storing negative stories, because I either change them or forget them.

Lalia: You seem like a perpetual learner. How does that help you?

Shar: I think that is my strength. At the end of the day, if nothing else happens, I am in it for the learning. That attitude of *I want to learn every moment and improve upon things* is something that pushes me forward.

Lalia: Do you have any goal-setting strategies that help you?

Shar: I plan my week every Sunday. I plan my month on the last day of the month before, as far as the events and conferences that I have to go to, so I don't miss out. I plan my meetings one week in advance. Every morning that I wake up, when I have my coffee or tea, I put a piece of paper in front of me and write a journal entry—basically, the things that I want to do. It helps me articulate it, and that, in turn, helps me to think of new things: *It would be amazing if I could do this!* Those are my goal-setting strategies.

Lalia: Do you ask yourself, *What is the ultimate reason for these goals?*

Shar: Yes, for sure. In terms of business, every month I plan in advance. For the week, I advance a general goal that I want to accomplish for the week. By looking at that general goal as a *why,* it helps me take the smaller steps. But that is also my weakness: I look into the *Why?* more than I think about the *What.* So, when I am setting goals, and I think of *why* something needs to be done, I get so absorbed into the *Why?* I lose out on figuring out the steps—the *What* that needs to be done.

Lalia: What do you think about risk? Entrepreneurs are considered risk-takers.

Shar: Yes, they are, but they do not embrace blind risk, like a lottery. It is about mitigating the bad results, figuring out a way to optimize the positive, and making sure to lessen the negative outcomes. The attitude of the entrepreneur is to be ready for the negative result, to plan for that to be in your attitude, to stand up to that, and to do whatever needs to be done to get a positive result.

Being ready to do something every day that I was scared of—that was a way for me to practice that risk-taking and get ready for it. You have to realize that, whatever happens, you are going to be good, and you can stand up again.

Lalia: When the way toward your goal is blocked, what do you do?

Shar: It always is. The way toward your goal is *always* blocked, and I would quote Rumi. "Step out, and the way appears. You don't have to see the way." You just have to understand what kind of resources you have. [Further], it's not even about *having* resources; it is about being resourceful with what you have, realizing and carrying the resources with you. It's never easy.

Lalia: I am using some of the positive-psychology research on grit and persistence and other mental strategies that help people get back up.

Shar: I got that. I don't think you learn any of that without going through hard times. You can always say, "What if I could shorten that time, with those tools? What if someone else could learn those tools?"

I think that, generally, for all of us in any business or any field that we are in, it is all about *the habits* that we have. For an entrepreneur, the biggest habit that they can build is the practice of being uncomfortable. The more fluent you get with being uncomfortable, the less probability you have of being depressed or scared of failing. Because you learn that you can always overcome. You don't learn unless you have gone through the hard times.

Key Strategies: Shar Behzadian

CREATE A STRUCTURE HACK

Shar credits her self-discipline both with helping to craft an overarching vision and with forging far-reaching goals. Relying upon established habits and techniques—"hacks," she calls them—for reminders, she keeps her sights trained on the tasks she wants to accomplish in both the immediate and the long term. A self-described "planner," she regularly structures her schedule on a daily, weekly, and monthly basis. As a way of enhancing her daily to-do lists, she employs a favorite hack—her colored wristbands. These help track her values, which are the main drivers behind each and every one of her goals.

SEEK OUT WISDOM

In addition to the everyday routines mentioned above, Shar also taps into deeper sources of wisdom, in particular, notable quotations from Rumi, the 13th-century Persian poet and mystic. Such insights have provided a deep confidence in her own internal resources. Indeed, it was only after reading Rumi that she first decided to follow her calling and create her own business.

You'll see this pattern repeated with frequency: It's not unusual for entrepreneurs to tap into ancient wells of philosophy, religion, or spirituality to usher them along their entrepreneurial path. Steve Jobs famously relied upon his experience with Zen Buddhism to guide his design principles. Lisa Fetterman also referenced a Zen and Stoic principle she uses to maneuver the various obstacles she encounters in both life and business.

BE A PERPETUAL LEARNER

According to Shar, she's in it for the learning. In fact, she considers this innate inquisitiveness, this questing nature, to be among her greatest assets. As a perpetual learner, she thrives on opportunities to grow as a person and entrepreneur. This quality helps foster her optimism and self-belief, too. Why? Because, regardless of outcome, she can take reassurance in the truism, "If nothing else happens, I am in it for the learning."

CULTIVATE FAITH, RESILIENCE, AND OPTIMISM

Ever the optimist, Shar finds comfort in the belief that she will be okay, no matter what. Like a cat, she will land on her feet. If one venture falls apart, she can forge ahead and build something else. It's that single kernel of faith—in herself, her ideas, and her skills—that carries her through countless trials and failures.

Despite her optimistic nature, Shar isn't naïve; she's not willfully blind to problems, potential risks, or the possibility of failure. Rather, she constantly seeks ways to transform negative outcomes into positive ones. For her, *all* things are doable. And in those rare moments of defeat, she has the mental strength to let it go, shrug it off, and begin searching around the bend for the next opportunity.

MINDSET EXERCISES

DESIGN YOUR OUTCOME

Using whiteboards or any writing surface, as well as online mind-mapping programs.

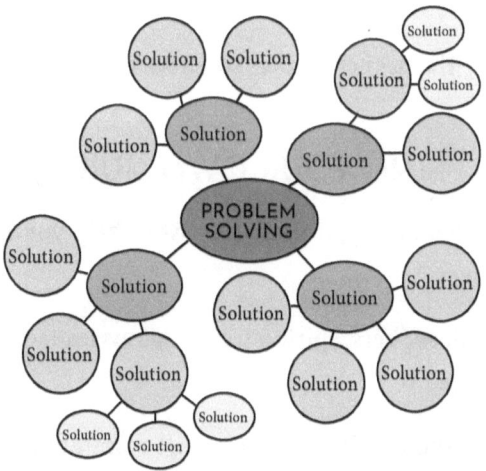

- Choose a difficult situation or problem that you are facing currently.
- Reframe it as the outcome you would like to have.
- Write down the outcome as the central topic, and place it in the center of your page or board.

- Generate associated ideas as your subtopics: What *needs* to be done? What *can* be done? What *has to happen* to achieve the outcome? (With brainstorming, even wild ideas can be considered.)
- Connect these subtopics to the main topics.
- For each of the subtopics, generate more ideas, and link them on the mind-map.
- You can get as creative as you want, using colors, graphics, etc.
- Allow yourself to move things around as you explore all your possible options.
- What are the next steps that you now know you need to take?

FIND YOUR OWN GUIDE

When you need an inspirational boost to help you get through your challenges.

- What philosophers, spiritual, or religious leaders have guided and inspired you?
- What are the ways you tap into that inspiration and wisdom in your work and daily life?
- Do you have a regular practice that gives you time for self-reflection?
- Do you have any personal philosophies that help you through the tough times?
- Do you take time to connect with nature, art, or music?

- How can you make it a habit—daily or weekly—to read from your favorite sources for inspiration and motivation?

TIME AND FOCUS

When you need help with staying focused by finding the right structure for time management.

- Identify your natural style for organizing yourself and managing your time. (Many people don't realize that their brains are predisposed to preferring structure or preferring flexibility.)
- Which time-management tools, methods, or habits have you experimented with?
- What aspects of them of them worked or didn't work?
- What are other possibilities that you could try?
- Do you prefer visual, auditory, or tactile cues to stay focused?
- Are there environments and spaces that work better for you? (E.g., some people enjoy the ambient noise of a coffee shop.)
- What kinds of rewards or accountability measures do you have in place for when you have achieved your goals?
- Where can you find more resources for time management and scheduling that you could use and implement?
- To understand more about your natural preferences, try some personality assessments that identify where on the scale of "structure" and "flexibility " you land.

You Either Hustle or You Give Up

ART AGRAWAL

Founder and CEO of YourMechanic

YourMechanic—a mobile car repair and maintenance service to customers at their location

Lalia: Tell me about what it's like to build a company.

Art: Building a company is hard for everybody, whether it's the first time, the second time, or the third. All of us can use a little boost, every now and then. Any ambitious project, like writing a book for the first time, can be daunting and motivating at the same time.

Lalia: The reason I'm doing this is that there is so much out there about being an entrepreneur that is really anecdotal. It doesn't necessarily look at what's going on in people's heads and how to make that work for you to get to that success.

I talked with Dr. Anu Basu, Professor and Director of Silicon Valley Center for Entrepreneurship about this. She is always fascinated by what makes entrepreneurs tick. In these entrepreneur programs at colleges and universities, they are not really addressing the psychology of entrepreneurs at all. They give courses on how to build a business, maybe some management courses, and some on how you build a team. But even in those courses, they are not getting those trait studies.

I think it's because people think that entrepreneurs are just born with this, so why study it? Not all are born that way; I think you are, maybe.

Art: I don't know if people are born with it. It was my circumstance that, in India, by nature, I think everyone is a businessman. That's a way of living. Every one of us is starting a business; someone is opening a shop; someone is opening a restaurant. Although, [I do think that] Americans are the most entrepreneurial of all; I'm thinking about all the innovations that are happening right here.

Lalia: Your presentation that I attended was titled "From Inspiration to Action." What is the mindset that you need? What are the things going on in your head—so that inspiration translates into action? At one point, you talked about how you dealt with the "… sh*t in your head." I want to talk about how to do this in a positive way.

So, let me start with a question about strengths. What are your strengths that are useful in being an entrepreneur?

Art: [The answer to this question would vary, depending on perspective:] Entrepreneur? Businessman? My strengths are that I could be very good at OPS, (operations), for example—that's very specific to the *business*. The terms that particularly define me as an *entrepreneur* are the ability to persist, no matter what happens, and also creativity.

We are in the business of innovation, so creativity is at the heart of it. You have to solve problems that are new—never have been before. But creativity is crucial to starting a new company in a new space. Also, by default, you have to be persistent, because, no matter how it looks from the outside, it is always messy on the inside. Look at a company like Uber. In three years, it became a billion-dollar company. But look at the inside: Uber has to deal with problems upon problems, the worst kind of problems that a start-up company has to deal with.

Travis (Kalanik) and his team are probably the only people on the planet who could have achieved what they have achieved. Even the best companies have sh*t inside. Even the best companies have everyday things that are not working—cars are on fire, governments are blocking them, and, still, they go on and build one of the best companies on the planet. I think if even the best have to face that, you can be sure that the rest of us have to be persistent to break through. I think that does apply in some sense.

Lalia: So, you think that your natural strength of creativity is useful in dealing with the problems?

Art: And coming up with solutions. Because you can go through the problems, or you really can create something meaningful. For example, with the problem of rescheduling, you can hire more people, or you can create a solution that really scales a business. I think that creativity is not just about solving a problem, but how you truly solve a problem to scale a business.

We are not running a mom-and-pop shop—you don't need a lot of creativity for a mom-and-pop business. You have to have creativity; you have to have resilience.

Lalia: How do you apply your strengths to your weaknesses? There are a couple of ways of dealing with them. Do you see your strengths as managing your weaknesses?

Art: I think I want to be focused on the things I want to be really good at. I don't want to focus on the things that I am bad at. For example, I am not good at managing people. I get impatient. I get aggressive. I have other people to deal with that. I can focus on the product, but I won't focus on customer service. Find someone else to do that.

Lalia: Yes—that's the theory: You focus on and build on your strengths, and you find ways to supplement your weaknesses with other people.

Lalia: Talk to me next about failure.

Art: There is not a badge in failure. The badge of honor is in winning; I guess they are trying to encourage a culture to take risks. But it doesn't make sense to me. If you're going to take risks, there are only two options: You are either going to win, or you are going to fail. There are no other options. You have to be okay with both options. If you are going to [be an] entrepreneur, you're jumping off a cliff: You are either going to die or survive. Don't say that's *okay*. Death is death—that's not okay. You have to be okay looking like a loser. I have experienced failure many times.

Lalia: What strategies do you use in your mind when you fail? What is in your head that says that it will be okay?

Art: What choice do you have? This is who I am. It's not about *okay*. The likelihood that you will succeed is very low, and the likelihood that you will make a lot of money is very low. So, it's not about prestige or being famous. You do it because you love it. If I fail to succeed, it doesn't matter. I know the consequences; I know my likelihood of success. I am okay taking those bets.

Lalia: You clearly have the willpower, the intrinsic motivation, to do this. How do you set goals for yourself?

Art: I don't wake up and say, "I need to make a million dollars a year." The way it has worked for me is: Let's figure out if there is a market opportunity, and let's launch a very small pilot. Let's start with two to three things and see what happens. I would go out and research a lot of ideas… it may take four to seven months—you just see what happens. You adjust your goals based on what you find out. It's a really methodical approach.

I have seen people set a lot of arbitrary goals: "I will make a million dollars by the end of next year." "I will start a business by the end of the year." How do you really know that? You want to break it down into specific steps. Over the last five years, I have learned to set smarter goals. Goals are arbitrary for some people. For me, planning is central. If I want to set a goal, I think through how I'm going to get there: *What steps am I going to take? What am I willing to sacrifice?* Let's say I want to run a marathon by next year. Do I realistically have the time for the training? Am I in a position to take these steps? People fail in their goals because they don't realistically think through their plans and their execution.

Lalia: Do you find that, when you're setting goals, you think about different options, just in case—like what things might fail or be obstacles? Do you look at these possibilities?

Art: Absolutely. There is a farmer analogy. You plant your seed; you grow your corn. There are external realities of life—there is going to be a spring and a summer, and you take into account the seasonality. I can't plan for everything. I want to be smart enough to say, "Under all the circumstances that I can think of, this is how I want to get there." Is it realistic? I want to be ambitious, but *realistically* ambitious. Planning is central for me. I think about the things I need to take care of.

Lalia: What are your thoughts about your personal effectiveness—what has contributed to your success as an entrepreneur?

Art: I think that maybe persistence is the single most important thing. It's not that I have brilliant ideas—or even the experience to do any of these things.

I didn't do a good job. If I went back now, knowing what I know, I would do a much better job. If I am not better today than yesterday, I am definitely not learning. So, I hope that, if I started YourMechanic today, because I have solved so many things that have happened over the last three years, I'd start it better. In that sense, the only thing that worked well for me was that I was willing to go through the things that I went through. I made lots of mistakes; it was okay, and I got through it.

Looking back, it's not surprising I failed. Timing is important. The ambitious mind thinks, *Timing doesn't matter.* That's not always true. Location, too. It's just about grit. You want to be smart. It isn't just about being persistent. You want to be smart; you've got to think through the feedback, as someone else has already seen all the problems. That was a big lesson I learned. I was too aggressive to listen to anyone. There were big lessons—they would have been *small* things, if I had taken the advice. It's a tricky balance between being persistent and knowing when to quit. It's not my life mission to fix cars, so I have to be careful about what I trade my time on. I am not getting this back. This had better be right.

Lalia: Here's a tricky situation, a question of balance: Persistence can flip into arrogance. What defines the point at which you know you have to quit?

Art: Sometimes your gut instincts are right—like the guy who built the wiper blade. He built something and persisted, and, eventually, he won. If you are an entrepreneur who is creating something that is new and exciting, you have to be very smart about how you spend time, because you could be solving some other thing. There's a very big tradeoff. This is time you are not going to be getting back, so this had better be right.

Lalia: Describe a positive event that has happened with your start-up.

Art: There are so many things. Working with awesome people is truly, well, *awesome*. Reading our customer reviews. It is such a joy to be here. Creating things that get lots of great reviews. We tried to raise money. We had $2 left in the bank. My cofounder said, "Let's just keep trying." Then we met someone who said, "Next job you get, you can pay me back." We found a backer. If we hadn't gotten all this support, we would not be here. There are fortunate moments.

Lalia: You talk about *luck*. Do you see any part that you personally play in *making* luck happen?

Art: You have to be out there for randomness to just happen. All these things have to happen while you are hustling. Although I believe that luck is about 90%, I believe that I have to be out there. I don't have a sales mindset. It was very hard for me to pick up the phone and call people I didn't know, but you have to do what you have to do. You just call and call and call, and you end up with the one phone call where they say: "You know, you're very persistent. You keep calling me, and I will meet with you." He could have been [some] creepy guy, so I was lucky in that. This job, to some extent, is doing things you don't like to do. So, yes, there is a lot of luck involved, but hustling accounts for about 10% of your success.

Lalia: Did you have any doubts along the way?

Art: There never was any question. There was no alternative. But what choice do you have? You either hustle or give up. Maybe there are moments, truly, at any point, where you can't see any way out, and the smart way [is to get] out. But, speaking for myself, I can't do that.

I have doubts probably three times a month. When you have a doubt, you have to ask yourself: *What are the things I have to do now? Is it time for me to make a choice about long-term outcomes? Where do I want to be fifty years from now? Is this really fitting with where I want to be?* If the answer is "No," then you should bail out.

Lalia: I see you as an intrinsically motivated human being.

Art: I'm not even sure that I'm highly motivated. Lots of people are very driven. The external things do not drive me. I just want to do things that I love. There are only a few things that I love.

I'm probably not an optimist, but neither am I am a pessimist. Maybe I am more a realist. I see the problems. Some things, I know I am going to overcome. I think it is slightly better to be an optimist.

■ ■ ■ ■ ■

Key Strategies: Art Agrawal

PERSISTENCE AND HUSTLE

It's a running motif throughout these conversations: The value of persistence. Art considers persistence one of his great strengths, and yet he remains mindful of the ways in which persistence can also prove a weakness if it edges into stubbornness. Indeed, Art cites his own stubbornness, his inability to heed feedback and re-tailor his approach, as a key factor in the failure of his previous ventures. Still, it's his persistence that helped shape his recent successes. By way of example, he recalls the way he relentlessly pursued investors despite his innate disinclination toward sales. As always, certainly, luck plays into the mix. For Art, though, a persistent sense of hustle may put you *in the path* of luck.

BUILD YOUR STRENGTHS AND COMPENSATE FOR WEAKNESSES

Art acknowledges his weaknesses—but he doesn't dwell on them. For instance, he mentions his limited customer-service skills. And while he could certainly improve on those abilities, such effort would be wasted when he could instead hire someone better equipped to handle those responsibilities.

A SENSE OF CLEAR-EYED REALISM

In Art's estimation, entrepreneurship offers only two outcomes—failure or success—and if you're going to take the risk, you'd better be okay with both. Yes, it's humbling to receive the pity of others, but, as Art says, "You have to be okay with looking like a loser." It's a blunt and brutal truism. At the same time, though, it's crucial to assess the potential for failure and the odds of success well in advance of launching your venture, as these assessments will guide your decision-making and help in preparing for the "shift."

PLANNING AND GOAL-SETTING ARE CENTRAL

Art believes that "people fail in their goals because they don't think through their plans and their execution." Buried within this idea is a shiny nugget of optimism: You can hack your way to success, in spite of all challenges, with the right sort of advance scoping. Art acknowledges that he has fine-tuned his own modes of goal-setting since starting YourMechanic.com. In particular, he strives to create much more concrete plans, with an eye toward avoiding arbitrary goals.

CULTIVATE A LEARNING MINDSET

Art strives to learn from all of his experiences, both the failures and the successes. He also derives great value from the lessons he acquires from more-experienced entrepreneurs. This openness toward learning has yielded a mindset that enables him to grow both as an entrepreneur and as a person. He's in good company, too. Many of the other entrepreneurs interviewed for this book noted the paramount importance of just such a mindset. According to psychologists, such perpetual learners exhibit a "growth mindset," rather than a "fixed mindset." For more information on this topic, check out the "Resources" section at the end of this book.

MINDSET EXERCISES

REALISTIC OPTIMISM

When you need a healthy boost of optimism, without giving up on reality.

- Think of a personal or business goal that you want to achieve.
- What are all the positive outcomes that can happen when you achieve this goal?
- What personal strengths have you used in the past to achieve a successful outcome?
- What are all the obstacles, challenges, and setbacks that you think you might confront?
- What skills, strengths, and resources have you used to overcome those challenges?
- What are the things that you can do to actively deal with the negatives and to turn them into better outcomes?
- What are the things that you can actively do to increase the chances for positive outcomes?

SET *SMART* GOALS

When you need to get back on track and get things done.

Specific What goal/s do you specifically want to achieve?

What are the steps you need to take to achieve this goal?

Measurable How are you going to measure each step you have taken?

How will you keep track of your progress?

Attainable Is this goal doable in your time frame?
What resources do you need?

What are the obstacles you may encounter?

Relevant Are your goals in line with your desired outcome?

What is the purpose behind these goals?

How does each step take you closer to fulfilling the purpose?

Time frame What is your time frame for achieving this goal?

DEAL WITH THE SH*T IN YOUR HEAD

When you need more self-confidence and help in reprogramming self-defeating thoughts and beliefs.

- Identify what your automatic negative thoughts are.
- Which of the thoughts include *should, must, can't, always*?
- Use a journal to capture those thoughts, and write out the negative "story" that you created about yourself.
- What behavior does having these negative thoughts and beliefs result in?
- What would be different if you didn't have these thoughts?
- Use these questions to challenge each of them:
    - What is the underlying belief here?
    - Is this actually true?
    - Is this always true?
    - When is this not true?
- What "more-truthful" thoughts can you replace this with that will be helpful?
- What is the story now?

If You Have Purpose, Everything Else Follows

MICHAEL COSCETTA

Vice-President of Global Sales at Square

> Square—a financial services and
> digital payments company

Lalia: I came in a little late to your talk, but you had mentioned Adam Grant, who is a really important figure in positive organizational psychology. I was just curious what the reference to him was about in that talk. Do you remember it?

Mike: I think it was about trying a lot of different things, because you very often recycle through a lot of bad things, or a lot of things fail before you actually get to the right one. And embracing the concept of failure. The old Edison quote—I'm sure it's misquoted, if he even ever said it—is: "I didn't fail however many thousand times to make a lightbulb. I just found out all the different ways not to make a lightbulb."

Lalia: My destination [with this book], just to give you a little context, is very much what you were referring to with Adam Grant. That is that, entrepreneurs, by the nature of the work they have to do, have to have—whether they're inherent or not—traits and mindsets that will allow them to achieve success in their ventures. Because you do have to be an original thinker. You do have to be creative. But in addition to that, you also need a lot of grit, persistence, and resilience.

Another thing that impressed me was what you said at that talk about positive energy and positivity. It's what the positive psychologists are trying to talk about. It's not just all optimism—you know, "everything's all wonderful" kind of stuff. But positivity is more about, instead of dwelling on the problems, it's about how you can create these positive energies in how you think and how you approach things.

I don't know if you would consider yourself an entrepreneur. I would. But you have worked with entrepreneurs, and you work in a start-up. I think you have some insight into the entrepreneur's mindset.

Mike: Yeah, I did own my own business for about nine and a half years as a start-up consultant, as a sales consultant. So, there's definitely an entrepreneurship *credibility* in me. I mean, did I go raise money and build a fully scalable global enterprise? No, I did not. It was my own thing, and I paid my own bills. Obviously, you're going to have the ups and downs along the way, but it's definitely one version of entrepreneurship. Not the same version that I think we see every day out here.

Lalia: Not the same version, but I'm also not focusing only on that. I have worked with and coached people in this situation—starting a consulting firm or some kind of an independent business on their own. So, I don't think that an entrepreneur's mindset is necessarily for somebody who's starting at an incubator kind of business. Because I think some of the issues are the same. I mean, my father was a doctor in the '50s and '60s, and he was unbelievably entrepreneurial. I think it's just that kind of a mindset where you see opportunity and understand how to overcome the challenges and move forward. So, how do you think of yourself as an entrepreneur?

Mike: I'll probably break it down into three different buckets. And this is kind of my scale of entrepreneurship for anyone.

One is: Did you start something yourself? Or are you willing to start something yourself and not walk into something that someone else has already built the foundation to? Because there's a whole different mentality and skill set, and, obviously, personality type—I mean *business* personality type—required for that foundation level, that ground layer. Even just the idea of coming up with the concept of a business is totally opposite to what it takes to refine or optimize an existing business.

The second is: I think the entrepreneur's mindset is something you already mentioned—which is a willingness and an ability to be agile. A willingness and a comfort with being right only 51% of the time. And to let other things slip and make mistakes and know you are not being perfect. You know you're not being efficient, but you're growing. So, within that, I think, is this growth mindset, and growth typically involves sacrifices and a willingness, again, to be comfortable with the uncomfortable.

The third thing is: The ability to create, sell, market, and sustain a vision. That is something that I feel is lost on many companies today. I believe it's one of the key reasons for failure. If you're going to get a person to join a two-person company, or a one-person company, or an eight-person company, there's tremendous risk there. One of the few ways of overcoming that risk is to actually have a compelling vision that motivates people. You almost create economic goodwill, where people *feel* like they're being paid for something when they're not, because they're contributing or being contributed to in a different way.

I think that vision is something that's very unique to an entrepreneur. If I draw that parallel that to myself, I was willing and able to start something on my own. Even at a very young age, I just liked the idea that I could make money without having to get a job or without having to rely on other people. [I've] always been in sales, and I've always enjoyed selling. I've always enjoyed the concept of: I could share something with other people that either caused them to be more focused, more excited, or more willing to do something than they were before.

Lalia: That's amazing. Thank you. You covered both yourself and also what you think is true for others. So, do you think that optimism is something that an entrepreneur needs to have? Would you describe yourself as an optimist?

Mike: I would say I've *become* one, only because I think I've seen the value. I think this goes back to the concept of creating a vision. Having vision means you're *selling the future.* You're creating this pathway in people's minds for how something will look, feel, sound, be perceived, be sold, be whatever. If, within that, you have pessimism, or skepticism, or frustration, or anxiety, that, of course, transfers to others—again, energy being the only true universal transferable currency. So, if you're trying to get people to do more, work harder, push themselves more, believe in more, they can't have that feeling of anxiety creep in or that feeling of uncertainty.

I think it's not just optimism—it's an ability to *sell* optimism, and it's an ability to get people to at least focus on the things going right, knowing full well there are still things going wrong and that it's okay. They're just part of the process; it's part of growth. It's part of, again, the Adam Grant concept of: *It's just another step closer to success.* Success is really just a lot of steps of failure in the process.

Lalia: What happens, though, when there are moments of doubt, when things look bleak, when there's, seemingly, almost no hope? What do you do? What have you seen other entrepreneurs do? How do they handle that within themselves and keep going?

Mike: There's a clear spectrum of people and how they react and how they embody confidence and beliefs. Some have just an absolutely single point in mind, a single-point intention. They don't see anything. They don't hear anything. They don't know anything except what they're looking at. They're able to completely tune out the world around them to focus on what they're doing, which can be good or bad, of course.

The second extreme, on the other side, is someone who's purely reactive and purely absorbent of the world around them. They see and hear and feel everything happening around them, so they actually forget where they're going. They spend a ton of energy; they end up on a hamster wheel, and they say, "Wow, I got so much done." But they really didn't get anything done because they actually weren't pointed in one direction. They get caught up in the doubts, and they change things a lot. They're freaking people out—they're giving direction in one way one day, and then they're giving a completely different direction the next day. Anytime energy is spent without progress [being made], it decreases confidence, because people don't feel that they're closer to a goal. They just feel like they've spent energy and haven't gotten anything or anywhere.

Between those two extremes, you have people who are willing and able to measure and monitor their ability to focus. One simple method people use is a daily to-do list. Checking before the day, checking at the end of the day. Someone asked that question at the event as well, and I think it's one of the most leverageable things you can do with younger employees, or at least newer employees. Give them goals at the beginning of the day, and check in at the end of the day. And, of course, do the same thing for yourself, when the day starts, and before the bullets fly. If, at the end of the day, you haven't done them, that means something else distracted you from what at the beginning of the day was the best set of things. It's always good to check back as to how many of those things you can still accomplish, despite the chaos and bullets flying throughout the day.

Having people who are self-aware enough to track that [is important]. You can also be robotic enough that you don't really need to be self-aware; you just have that regimen—whether it pops up on a Google Calendar or a Post-it note on your computer or your desk.

I think the next level of that is having peers, or, at least, trustworthy people who can keep you in line and keep you on track when you're not focused, or when you're not being positive, when you are focusing more on the negative and the challenges than the things that are going right. That can be someone inside of the company; it can be someone outside the company. I think there's value in both, because, obviously, someone inside knows what's going on and probably what should be done. Someone outside, though, is usually more objective and can have a little more of a big picture in their analysis, versus just thinking within the confines of that individual business, or that day, or that person.

The next level above that is someone who is very quick to catch him or herself when they are starting to get frustrated and when they are starting to feel off track. Think of two parallel lines. If you make one very, very minor adjustment to one and you extrapolate that over time, that, of course, becomes a very large deviation from expected destination to actual destination. It's about being able to get back on track as soon as possible, whether it be through check-ins with mentors, check-ins with peers, weekly product updates, weekly product reviews, whatever. The simplest way we do it now is to ask: *What are my objectives, and what are the key results to get me there?* And do a weekly, biweekly, monthly, quarterly, annual check-in on all those things, because that's the easy way, and you keep it solely red, yellow, or green. Keep it ultra-, ultra-simple. The more detailed people have to go, the more they get caught up in the detail, and, again, the quicker they lose sight of where they are.

The last thing is that people typically will sacrifice themselves for their business. And, again, there's a tipping point there, beyond which—no matter how much you put into your business—if you're not contributing back to yourself, physically, mentally, emotionally, spiritually, everything, you will have nothing left to give. It's like a car engine that's [running] on fumes. You can slam that gas pedal down as hard as you want, but there's nothing there to combust anymore. There's no more energy to be produced.

It's that concept of *energy*—showing up every single day with more energy than every person around you, and having someone ready, willing, and able to call you out when they notice that you're not being the same person that you were.

Lalia: Yeah, that's great. I mean, you're back to explaining about positive energy, which I really love, and you're talking about how to regenerate that in yourself.

Can I ask you to give me a personal example? When you confronted some doubts or some obstacles that sank you in a way, how did you get yourself back up to that positive energy that you needed to move forward?

Mike: I'm trying to think of a clear example that makes sense and that also doesn't take too long to explain. So, a few years ago, a very good friend, who was chief of staff to the CEO, asked me to help create a sales program for a cloud-based company. This was a friend of mine who had worked for me previously, so there was credibility between him and me. There clearly wasn't [yet] credibility between me and the CEO.

It just took a very long process of sitting down with him, almost on a daily basis, and giving him updated points of progress—where the team was progressing, where people [customers] were starting to buy, and where we had developed a training program. We now had different people doing different things and succeeding, even though they had spent four years in their previous role and were very locked in.

I didn't deliver him anything perfect, but, every day, I over-communicated, and I over-shared, until the point where he said, "Listen, I appreciate that you're doing this, but I don't need you to do this. If there's a problem, let me know. If you need my help, let me know. But come back in two weeks, and let's revisit." At that point, I knew I had trust. Within trust, I was able to then refocus and keep myself on track as opposed to being paranoid every day that I wasn't doing enough or that I wasn't up to standards.

Lalia: It actually parallels really well with what some psychologists define as optimism, which is that, when things are going badly, the optimist has the belief that there is something that they can do—that there is something you can control—and you take action around that. You don't fall victim to the bad things. In other words, you don't say, "Oh, my god—this always happens to me. I'm a failure." Which is how a pessimist would look at it: "This is true for everything I do" kind of thing. The optimist's view is, "This isn't my fault, this stuff happening. But I have control over something around this situation, and I can do something about it."

Mike: There's a component of control there. Right? Which is so important. That, even if you don't have control, [you have] the feeling that you have control. Or the ability to influence enough to where you know that, if you just put enough energy behind it, you can actually muscle something through. That's a very empowering place for people to be, because, again, it proves that there's a system.

Lalia: It's empowering to have that. In many cases, people do not have that mindset. One of the other things I found with entrepreneurs is that they have a real understanding of what their strengths are. They don't bother with building up their weaknesses. They hire the people they need to offset their weaknesses, because it's not the best use of their time and energy to do the things that they don't do well. How do you view that for yourself personally?

Mike: There's a lot that I'm aware I'm not good at. I think there's the stages of *conscious* confidence and *unconscious* incompetence, and all those stages of learning. I think the more you know, the more you know you don't know. There's a comfort in not being perfect and knowing that there's this large world out there. Not until you do certain things do you start to learn and realize certain things about yourself.

I think there's a component of self-awareness of what you're good at and what you're not good at. And a lot of that just takes time. I think there's also just an awareness component of *other people who will help you* be very conscious of what you're good at and what you're not good at. [You have to] trust that they're doing it for objective reasons, not for personal reasons. A personal weakness is not a personal insult—it's just, again, that there's a finite amount of time and energy in the day, and it's not always possible to put time into everything.

For me, it's relying on external forces at first to help build that set of skills—help build that awareness of what's there and what's not there. I had a coach very early in my career who convinced me that I have an incredible ability to get a gut reaction to something as opposed to a cerebral reaction to something. There is an actual biochemical underpinning to that. Your gut is where all neurotransmitters typically direct their first attention for your sympathetic or parasympathetic nervous system. The first place your nervous system touches is in your digestive system—which was, at least to me, not something I understood. I have been learning to rely on my gut more, learning to rely on my instincts more.

The power of intention is another strength of mine. When I told myself I would do something, at some point, it figured itself out—whether it be the universe, whether it be God or Jesus Christ, or anything. I don't know. But I do know that if I look back on my life—on the times when I really focused on something—the amount of times I failed were very, very few. Relying on that confidence—that, if you believe it, it'll somehow force itself into reality.

I know I have plenty of weaknesses. I like to make fun of them. There's a comfort that comes with knowing I have weaknesses. I know I have specific words I say in sentences over and over again when I speak in public. I know I've got a big nose and big ears. I know I love to talk, and I'm terrible at keeping myself on time in messages. I know that I probably spend way too much money on traveling and food, and those are fun things. At the same time, I know where I'm weak in relationships. I know where I'm weak spiritually. Part of it is just the objective decision-making: Is this worth my time to pursue? Or is it an overuse of time, and I'm just going to get diminishing returns in doing so?

Lalia: When you worked with entrepreneurs, how do you see that they deal with their strengths and weaknesses?

Mike: I think it depends where they are in their life. One of my heuristics is that, the younger someone is, the less aware of their weaknesses they probably are. Is that positive or negative? Depending on who they are, what they're doing, it could be either. As they get older, I think people become naturally more aware of their weaknesses because they experience more. So, there's a longer list of baggage in their head that they're carrying with them.

For me, it's how quickly can I get to that understanding of which of those four buckets they're in: Young in their career, later in their career, aware, not aware. Once I kind of understand that, it gives me a little bit better direction as to how much time *they* want to spend on their weaknesses, and how much time *I* think they need to spend on their weaknesses.

If someone's about to go raise money, and they do not exude confidence, think agilely, prepare proper financial information, or pay attention to detail, they need to be aware [of that]. They need to hire someone to do that with them or for them—or else this is going to be a major issue for them.

A lot of people are willing to learn, but it depends on time. Do they have enough time? I think if someone's [younger] and they're building a bigger company or managing more senior people, are they aware of their legitimate weaknesses as a leader? If you're a leader, perception is everything, since you're potentially younger in your career and might be managing people who've done this fifteen different times. How do you address them? When do you address them? Do you do it with self-deprecation? Do you do it with humor? Do you compensate with consultants? Do you hire leadership coaches?

There's gotta be some reward for you throughout the process of having made that progress—whether it be just recognition, or introductions to different people, or we go out and celebrate that they raised that round, because they did XYZ. I, of course, as the coach, want to align myself as much as possible with those successes, but I also want them to know that the success happened only because of their commitment, their sacrifice, and their focus on having grown themselves some way.

Lalia: Great. That's a great answer.

Mike: I still don't know what I think of Mark Buckingham's book [*Now, Discover Your Strengths*]. They're so detailed in how many strengths they list. The fact that they actually isolate them, I think, is interesting enough to people who might not have ever thought about their strengths or weaknesses previously. Sometimes even the exercise of having people dig into [their strengths] is eye-opening enough to get them excited to grow as a person for the next twelve months.

I really believe part of the sales pitch I put on for any leader, any entrepreneur, is just a personal-growth exercise. Even if they don't grow their business, if they don't grow their finances, if they don't grow anything, they grow as a person, and that will pay dividends many years into the future in ways that they can't even comprehend. I want people as excited about *that* growth as any type of financial or business growth.

Lalia: I would certainly high-five you on that one. That's where I'm trying to go with all of this.

Lalia: I'm going go a little bit back to goals, because you started out talking about that. There's this concept that *there's always hope if you can see an alternative.* You know, the "Plan B." I've asked entrepreneurs I've interviewed, *Do you have a "Plan B" when you're setting up with objectives?* They have to know that the chances are pretty high that things are going to not go the way they were thinking they would.

Mike: See, I think it depends on how you define "Plan B." Is it a Plan B for the company, or is it a Plan B for achieving the goal? Is it a different method, a different path? Or is it just, "Oh, sh*t! If this fails, I'm just going to do something else," and having something else in their mind?

For me, it's the concept of an alternative plan or an alternative path, not always just a fallback. I think some people might view a Plan B as a fallback, which—in entrepreneurial circles—is actually like a four-letter word. You hear everyone who becomes mega-successful in a sport or something very unique say, "Oh, I never had a fallback. I just always knew I wanted to be a baseball player from the day I was born." Whether that's true or not, I think, is up for debate, but

I've found that, if people have Plan B's, they very often have Plans C through Z. But they're able to ignore all of them for Plan A.

For whatever reason, something switches, their amygdala kicks in, you know, a shot of epinephrine hits their heart, choline hits their brain and says, "Oh, sh*t! We need to scramble. We need to figure something out." Everyone calls them *the OSMs*—right, the *Oh, sh*t! Moments*—but some people need an *Oh, sh*t! Moment* to get there. Some people need an external factor or an objective consultant to come in and say, "Hey, I just want you to know, I think it's really important that we look at an alternative here."

Lalia: Right. An alternative. Yeah. It goes back to the sense of knowing that you'll always have some kind of choice. Is it valuable to assume that things can go wrong? And to plan for that?

Mike: Yes. Absolutely. I think if you don't, you're flying by the seat of your pants. Maybe you'll be lucky. Maybe whatever you think of in that moment is exactly what needed to happen, but I would also assume nine times out of ten that what you do in a reactionary sense would probably be the wrong thing.

Lalia: Ashton Kutcher said that there's only one thing he looks for when he's investing in somebody, in a start-up, and that's how much grit the founder has. How do you view grit, persistence, and the necessity of that for an entrepreneur?

Mike: I really wish I had a way of quantifying it. Because I really believe it's one of the most important things, if not *the* most important thing. How I define *grit* is that it's a willingness to do more. It's a willingness to do something different. It's a willingness to be this subservient employee. It's a willingness to sweep the floor or clean the bathrooms, if you absolutely need to get the job done. It's a willingness to work harder. It's a willingness to think on your feet. It's a willingness to persist through trouble and through problems. I think there are proxies for grit. I think there are proxies for just that resiliency; to me, they go hand in hand. I think anyone who's resilient has grit. If they have one, they always seem to have the other.

Lalia: Let's say you were advising an entrepreneur and they were facing a lot of hardship and struggling and really getting low. You say to them, "Well, you just have to have more grit—you have to have more persistence." What if they say, "Yeah, but how do I find that in myself?" What would you say?

Mike: I think the first reaction to any type of adjustment should be undertaken in a very linear, very methodical kind of way. You create a list of things to do [every day] and just start by checking the stupid boxes and saying, "Okay—you told me I have to eat five carrots a day. I ate five carrots a day. Now what?" I don't think that's going to get someone very far, but at least they know what that means, and there's an established definition of *grit*.

The second is: Once someone has the specific steps, they have to know *why*. The steps are the skeleton, and the *why* is the body around it—the skin, and the hair, and the color, and everything that gives it real life. If they don't understand the *why*, then, of course, eventually, within a few days, they've stopped doing the *what*. So, they have the steps, and they have the *why*. I think that's a coach's responsibility or someone else's responsibility—maybe a girlfriend or boyfriend. It could be their husband or wife. It could be a professional. It could be their cat. Someone has to keep them in the loop as to *why this is important*.

The third thing is: You need to track the quick progress. There has to be something tangible to be delivered as a result of doing those steps. If there aren't tangible results within a short period of time, I think people very quickly lose faith, because they just don't see the progress necessary to feel accomplishment.

The fourth thing is: You have to then take a step back as that coach and see if the stuff can now persist on its own. Does the person stay within that mindset and that path? Or do they immediately revert back to doing whatever it was that they were doing? There has to be a check mechanism back to saying, "No, you're doing this again." I think, over time, they end up owning it, and they end up owning at least the progress made through that point.

But they have to realize that *grit* is more about a *willingness* to do something—it's not the *actual doing* of it. If I see that the garbage needs to be taken out—and it's typically my assistant's job to do it, but I saw it was full—I tie it up, and I walk it out to the dumpster. That makes a really big difference to people. They see that, and they think, "Oh, crap! He didn't ask me to do it. He just did it himself." That tells them it's important. I think part of what a leader does is that what they spend time on, what they spend energy on, is a signal to other people of what's important.

So the tasks that show *grit* are very often the things that might be very low-level, but they might be ultra-, ultra-important to the growth of the business. Other people need to see them doing it. Other people need to see that it's important. They have to know that it's so important that even the CEO is now doing XYZ, and showing enthusiasm and energy for doing it—not that they're stepping in to steal someone's time or energy, or steal the spotlight. And that's where I think the *why* comes in as well.

Lalia: That is also another thing that I've found—you know, uniformly. There's a real sense of purpose behind what the founders I've talked to are doing, and that provides an enormous motivation to continue and to just keep going.

Mike: You said it starts with *why*, right? If you have purpose, everything else follows.

■ ■ ■ ■ ■

Key Strategies: Michael Coscetta

IT'S A PROCESS

One of the three criteria of an entrepreneur's mindset that Mike mentioned was being agile. Part of being agile is being willing to make mistakes and not seek perfection, so that can you change direction when you need to. Mike also warned about the dangers of stubbornness—*not* changing course when, clearly, you are on the wrong one.

It's important to seek forward movement, progress, and getting better and better. Others in this book have mentioned this same aspect of the "growth mindset" and the importance of continuing to learn, improve, and grow. They don't expect things to work out perfectly or to accomplish everything all at once. Instead, progress is a *path*.

While there is a lot of learning from failures, there is learning from progress, too. Mike assesses progress with documentation, marking what's been achieved and what could have been done differently. Mike makes sure, when coaching or consulting others, as well as for his employees and himself, that both small and big progress deserves to be celebrated. That act of celebration becomes a strong motivator to continue on the path.

HOW TO GET GRIT—THE WHAT AND THE WHY

Mike sees grit and resilience as one of the most important traits that an entrepreneur needs. He believes that one of the key strategies to staying persistent is to set goals, create lists, and maintain markers—so that, when things go bad, there is a structure to fall back on. Knowing *what* you have to do on those lists, including all the junky stuff, like taking out the trash and sweeping the floors—*as well as* making the day-to-day business decisions—are anchors that get you back on track and keep you focused.

This gets one just so far unless there is a big *why* behind these goals and tasks. Mike is a big believer that having a vision and purpose is an important factor in powering up persistence. Without it, that commitment can falter after you've taken out the trash for the hundredth time, and there's little motivation left for the really important work to be done. Having that vision will pump up positive energy and enthusiasm to motivate you and will infect those around you as well.

CONTRIBUTE BACK TO YOURSELF

Mike and I talked about the importance of maintaining energy as an entrepreneur. You can't expect to survive when you use up all of your energy by pouring it into your business venture. You have to look out for your health—mental, physical, spiritual, personal. He equates this to a car, which is your overall well-being—it needs fuel. That fuel needs to be replenished with sources other than working 24/7.

TAKE CONTROL OF WHAT YOU CAN

In Mike's story about project-consulting for a CEO, you can see how he overcame a challenging situation and when he was close to losing the job. He made a conscious choice to take control of the problem by taking meaningful action. He assessed where he could exert the most influence and where he could perform at his best.

By *way over-delivering* on the CEO's expectations, Mike secured the CEO's trust and confidence and, more importantly, created enormous value for the company's future.

PERSONAL GROWTH PAYS DIVIDENDS

Of all the entrepreneurs I met, Mike was the most knowledgeable about the key concepts of positive psychology that permeate my interviews. With Mike having read several of the books and authors mentioned, it was easy for us to have a free exchange of ideas around personal development and how they applied to the mindset of an entrepreneur.

He is a believer that learning about one's own strengths and weaknesses can be an exciting part of one's personal growth and self-development. Regardless of whether a person achieves success in a particular endeavor, the personal growth acquired by knowing one's strengths and weaknesses will "pay dividends" for many years into the future.

Mike gave an example of one of his strengths—really good gut instincts— that have paid dividends by giving him greater self-confidence in making decisions and judgments.

MINDSET EXERCISES

FOCUS ON YOUR CIRCLE OF CONTROL

When you need to be more empowered and proactive in a challenging, stressful, or overwhelming situation.

- Draw three concentric circles on a piece of paper.
- Above the three circles, write down your biggest worry or concern.

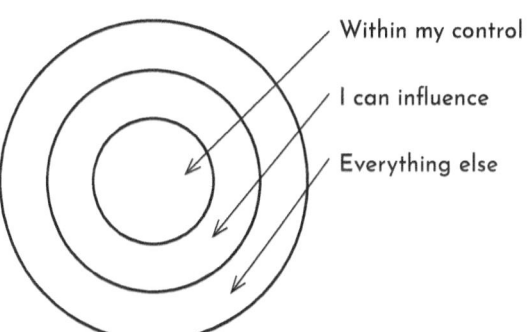

- Assign each of them with the following:
    - Innermost circle—within my control
    - Interior circle—I can influence
    - Outermost circle—everything else

- Write down for each circle:
    - What are the things in this situation that are within my control?
    - What are the things in this situation that I can influence?
    - What are things that I perceive as not having any control over, and what are the things I am certain I don't have any control over?
- For each circle, write down some action items that will help you have more control or influence.
    - What are the next steps to take in the areas where I have control?
    - What are some steps that I can take to positively influence or change an outcome?
    - What are the next steps to take when I can't change the outcome but possibly can find some control over?

INVEST IN YOURSELF

It will pay dividends.

- How can you pay more attention to your needs—physical, emotional, mental, spiritual?
- Where can you find opportunities for self-discovery? E.g., reading, coaching, feedback from others, mentoring.
- How can you get more energy in a positive way?
- What types of activities boost your creativity?

- What can you do to achieve more balance in your life?
- How can you develop the relationships that you need to help you?
- How can you give yourself permission to take a break?
- How will investing in your well-being help you achieve your goals?

BOUNCE BACK FROM SETBACKS

When you are feeling ready to throw in the towel and give up!

- What coping strategies have you used in the past when you have experienced problems, challenges, difficulties, or failures?
- Which of these strategies would best serve you right now?
- What strengths have you used in the past to help you get through difficulties?
- Which of these can you tap into now?
- What new strengths that you have discovered can you use to overcome this challenge?
- How can your support system help you at this time?
- What are the actions you can take toward solving some aspect of the problem?
- What is within your control right now?

BRING IT ALL TOGETHER

Your personal SOAR analysis (for more information, please refer to the Resources section).

The questions in the boxes are merely suggestions to guide you in this discovery. You can use the answers from other questions in the book to pull together your learnings and create an overall strategy to further develop your *Entrepreneur's Mindset*.

STRENGTHS	OPPORTUNITIES
What have you learned about your strengths? What do you do well, what are your resources, and what personal strengths can you build upon?	Where do you see opportunities for success? What are some of the obstacles that can be turned into opportunities? How can you find the opportunities?
ASPIRATIONS	**RESULTS**
Where would you like to see yourself in the future? What are the goals and outcomes you want to achieve? What are you excited about for yourself or for your business that you see ahead of you?	What goal/s are you committing to? How will you measure and reward your progress and achievement? How will you feel about the process and the outcome? Now, what action will you take to achieve your best outcomes?

CONCLUSION

Each of the entrepreneurs I interviewed has struggled along their path. They have taken knocks, each of them, and rebounded. You can hear the intensity of effort in their sentences; you can sense the sweat and labor behind their tone. But they have also found great optimism and joy in their individual journeys. They have learned from their failures, thrilled to their victories, and toasted their milestones.

Much to our benefit, too, they have strengthened their mindsets along the way, gathering bits of wisdom, as they launched and grew their numerous businesses. As I conducted these interviews and revisited these pages over and over, I have sifted through their words to pluck out the brightest gems of advice, but there are surely many more nestled within each conversation. Likely you have found some of them. I hope you have, certainly.

It's fascinating to cross-reference their remarks, too. There's insight to be found in the individual pearls of advice—the unique ones, spoken by one interviewee and unmentioned by the others—but there is also deep wisdom in the overlap of ideas. No doubt you have noticed several consistent messages: optimism, resilience, the value of failure. These themes and others, too, echo throughout the words of our entrepreneurs.

I have also offered you some mental tools to hone your own entrepreneur's mindset. These exercises are based on what positive, social, and cognitive psychologists sometimes call "interventions."

Included within the exercises are the types of questions often used by coaches, counselors, and mentors to aid a client or mentee in their self-discovery and development. My hope is that the exercises and their questions are framed in a way that enables you to "self-coach" yourself, thereby enabling your own process of self-discovery.

Some exercises may resonate with you more than others. Some may be more adaptable to your situation than others. Whether you choose to engage with these exercises by simply reflecting on the questions or decide to write out full answers in a journal, I suspect you will derive considerable benefit from using them. In fact, by engaging with the exercises in a conscious, consistent manner, you will create positive mental habits that can inform your endeavors far into the future.

A longtime friend and successful serial entrepreneur once remarked to me that if he obtained one single piece of useful advice from a personal-development book, class, or workshop, it was well worth the effort. If you have arrived at this last chapter, I suspect you have acquired at least one bit of valuable advice (hopefully more!). Perhaps, you too, have been inspired to persevere in your own entrepreneurial ventures, or maybe you have gained a renewed belief in yourself. If so, then my objective as stated in the introduction, has been fulfilled.

Kudos to you for taking this step toward knowing yourself better and honing a stronger, more positive mindset—that of a true entrepreneur. Indeed, never doubt that you have what it takes to succeed.

Best of luck, and may you find joy in the journey!

ACKNOWLEDGMENTS

I wish to start by thanking my husband, Hamilton, for his support and encouragement in this and all of my endeavors. I could not have begun, let alone finished a project like this without his absolute conviction in my ability to pull this off, even in my greatest moments of doubt. He is my support, rock, and guide in all things that matter.

I would also like to thank my children, Margaret, Edmund, and Andrew, along with their spouses and partners, Blair, Cara, and Peris, and their beautiful little boys, who have been the lights of my life. There is no greater reward than having them as my cheerleaders, providing me with the self-confidence and determination to pursue my own dreams.

I am especially grateful to my son-in-law, Blair Kroeber, a brilliant writer in his own right, who has provided me with much-needed editorial guidance and inspiration for this book.

With gratitude to the following entrepreneurs who made this book possible. (Current positions are listed here.)

Art Agrawal, Founder of Jerry.ai and YourMechanic.com

Shar Behzadian, CEO at Immersive City Tales

Michael Coscetta, Chief Commercial Officer and Chief Strategy Officer at Compass; Angel investor and start-up advisor

Lisa Fetterman, VP of Operations at Constellation Agency

Greg Kimma, CFO at InstaMaids

Duncan Logan, Former Chief Strategy Officer at Nex Cubed; Board Member at Renaissance, Nex Cube; Advisor at Sway Ventures, Hostfully

Iddo Tal, Founder of Raise the Round; PM lead @ Google

Guy Praisler, Founder and CEO of Dine Market; Partner at Mejix Inc.

RESOURCES

CONFIDENCE/SELF-EFFICACY
Bandura, Albert. *Self-Efficacy: The Exercise of Control.* 1997.

Jewell, Louisa. *Wire Your Brain for Confidence: The Science of Conquering Self-Doubt.* 2017.

GOALS
Halvorson, Heidi Grant. *Succeed: How Can We Reach Our Goals?* 2011.

GRIT
Duckworth, Angela. *Grit: The Power of Passion and Perseverance.* 2018.

GROWTH MINDSET
Dweck, Carol S. *Mindset: The New Psychology of Success.* 2008.

OPTIMISM
Seligman, Martin E. P. *Learned Optimism: How to Change your Mind and Your Life.* 1991.

RESILIENCE
Reivich, Karen and Andrew Shatté. *The Resilience Factor.* 2002.

SOAR

Stavros, Jacqueline and Gina Hinrichs. *The Thin Book of SOAR*. 2nd edition, April 15, 2019.

STRENGTHS

Buckingham, Marcus, and Donald O. Clifton, *Go Put Your Strengths to Work: 6 Powerful Steps to Achieve Outstanding Performance*. 2001.

Niemiec, Ryan M., and Robert McGrath. *The Power of Character Strengths: Appreciate and Ignite Your Positive Personality*. 2019.

Rath, Thomas. (Gallup) StrengthsFinder 2.0. 2007.

THINK "DIFFERENTLY"

Grant, Adam. *Originals: How Non-Conformists Move the World*. 2016.

BIOGRAPHY

M. Lalia Helmer is an executive leadership coach who helps individuals, teams, and organizations to flourish. Her work facilitates creative, interactive programs and workshops that inspire attendees toward greater understanding of and collaboration with others. An undergrad professor of Business Psychology with a diverse range of clients worldwide, Ms. Helmer lives in the San Francisco Bay area. Her greatest passions are her family, dancing, travel, and hiking.

You can contact her at: linkedin.com/in/laliahelmer and find more information on www.laliahelmer.com

www.ingramcontent.com/pod-product-compliance
Lightning Source LLC
Chambersburg PA
CBHW030908080526